T0266002

Asperger's and Self-Esteem

Insight and Hope through Famous Role Models

Norm Ledgin

Foreword by
Dr. Temple Grandin

Illustrations by Marsha M. Ledgin

FUTURE HORIZONS INC.

All marketing and publishing rights guaranteed to and reserved by

FUTURE HORIZONS INC.

721 W. Abram Street
Arlington, Texas 76013
817-277-0727
800-489-0727
817-277-2270 (fax)
E-mail: info@FHautism.com
www.FHautism.com

Copyright 2002 by Norman M. Ledgin

All rights reserved.

Inside art, Copyright 2001 by Marsha M. Ledgin

Foreword, Copyright 2001 by Temple Grandin

Printed in the United States of America

No part of this book may be reproduced in any manner whatsoever without written permission of Future Horizons, Inc., except in the case of brief quotations embodied in reviews.

Cataloging in Publication Data is available from the Library of Congress.

ISBN 978-1-935274-62-9

*To my first-born, Stephanie Paula Ledgin-Toskos,
who eased me into a new form of work at a late
stage in my life—the writing of historical
observations to raise gifted young people with
Asperger's Syndrome from self-doubt.*

*And to a great teacher who prefers to be known
only as "Kanga," for encouraging me—with the
right measures of enthusiasm, counsel, and
wisdom—toward undertaking and completing this
particular work*

ASPERGER'S AND SELF-ESTEEM

Contents

Preface

Welcome to a new way of looking at historical figures—successful people who had tendencies or traits shared by persons now diagnosed with Asperger's Syndrome, or high-functioning autism.

This is not psychohistory or analysis of why famous people behaved as they did. Think of this book as matching reliable observations of them with a diagnostic matrix available today. The study provides insight into their successes and helps explain personal failures.

Some of the names may surprise you, because they are those of men and women who have made significant contributions to our lives and in that respect may be role models for the young. Yet in many instances they contributed without understanding, recognizing, or even caring about the mechanics of social relationships. Interactions that come naturally to you and me were, to a varying extent, a mystery to the majority of them.

Because these figures are all dead, we can never know whether all would have met the classic definition of Asperger's Syndrome. Unquestionably, however, they all shared many characteristics of the condition, yet they made significant marks in history.

Research for this book was done carefully in the spirit of the study, *Diagnosing Jefferson.* You can verify facts and quotations about the principals in sources listed at the end of this book. All author's conclusions are based upon modern theory or fact.

Please examine both the challenges and benefits of Asperger's as you read this. Yours will be an interesting journey into a new perspective.

Norm Ledgin

Foreword
by Temple Grandin

High school was torture for me. I was the weirdo all the "cool" kids teased. When I crossed the parking lot, they would yell "Bones!" because I was skinny, and "Tape Recorder!" because I was always repeating myself.

Norm Ledgin's book would have been very helpful to me when I was a teenager. It would have boosted my self-confidence to know that famous scientists and musicians had many of the same problems I was having. The kid who is "big man on campus" in high school is seldom the person who makes a big contribution to society when he grows up. The nerdy, picked-on kid is the one who later develops new computer technology or makes a great discovery.

A dedicated high school science teacher rescued me from the nightmare of teasing. He became a mentor, working with me to develop my scientific interests even after I started college. In my first two college years I visited his lab almost every weekend. Mr. Carlock's science lab was a refuge from the teenage social world I did not understand, and my work in his lab motivated me to study. Before that I had been a poor student, bored and unmotivated.

Today I have a satisfying career that has given my life meaning and made life worth living. I am successful as an animal behavior specialist and designer of cattle-handling facilities. Half the cattle in the United States and Canada are handled in chute systems I have designed. I am also on the animal science faculty of Colorado State University.

Many people thought I would never amount to anything because I was diagnosed with autism. Some educators thought I was retarded and would achieve very little. Not everyone understands that autism and Asperger's Syndrome are neurological conditions a child is born with, nor is it generally understood that autism contains a continuum of traits from normal to abnormal. I was diagnosed with autism because I had delayed speech. Children diagnosed with Asperger's are a milder variant, and speech development is usually within the normal range. Asperger's children are usually identified when they have social problems in the third or fourth grade. They are the lone children who have few friends.

Another phenomenon of Asperger's is that there is no sharp line dividing the syndrome from people who are "computer nerds." The December 2001 issue of *Wired* magazine reported a higher incidence of autism and Asperger's in communities containing many people in computing and technology fields. During countless autism conferences I have observed that autistic and Asperger's traits are often present to a milder degree in parents and relatives. There is a strong inherited basis for autism. Researcher Simon Baron-Cohen of England has found the family history of people with autism or Asperger's contains significantly more engineers. This was certainly true in my family. My grandfather on my mother's side was a shy, quiet engineer who invented the automatic pilot for airplanes. Engineers and mathematicians are on both sides of my family. My first cousin's son is a top circuit-board designer, and there is musical and artistic talent in my mother's family.

Importance of Developing Talents

The skills of children with high-functioning autism or Asperger's Syndrome are often uneven. They can be gifted in one area and do poorly in another. I excelled at memorizing and at such visual skills as drawing and designing. I am a visual thinker, and when I design equipment I can test-run it in my head like a virtual-reality computer. My deficit is that I cannot do abstract math such as algebra. Hours of algebra tutoring were useless, and as a result I was never given the opportunity to study geometry. For many Asperger's children, however, numbers represent a strong skill—math and music. With few exceptions they are unable to do tasks requiring visualization such as drawing.

Giftedness tends to fall into two types of minds when skills are uneven—either a visual-thinking mind like mine or a math and music mind, and each shows opposite shortcomings. I am good at drawing and visualizing, and the person with the music and math mind is often poor at drawing. Furthermore, those with music and math minds frequently excel at computer programming.

Often there is too much emphasis on deficits or weaknesses–not enough on developing areas of strength and talent into skills that can provide careers.

People respect talent. The only times I was not teased in high school were when I worked with other students on projects of shared interest. Mr. Carlock ran the model rocket club, and when we were making rockets the other kids did not tease me. Horseback riding was another activity where the teasing stopped. The other students appreciated my skills in building model rockets or making fancy show bridles for horses. Teasing, however, occurred during purely social times such as lunch or congregating in the parking lot, and it came from socially "cool" kids who were not part of the rocket club or horse shows.

Talents should be developed into skills that can provide satisfying careers. And a satisfying career also provides opportunities for having good friends through shared interests. Many students in the rocket club were the little nerdy kids who were teased or picked on at lunch. I fit in really well with this group!

Today my best friends are in careers where we have shared interests. Some of the best times of my life have come through shared interests. I love getting into deep, intellectual discussions about animal behavior. I have had great times with my engineer friends. The intellectual stimulation of figuring out how to invent a new piece of equipment is great fun. I have spent hours with engineering friends discussing different designs for meat plants or feedlots. We are "into" the details. We have a good time discussing details of the good and bad points of each design. My social life revolves around people with whom I share interests. Idle chit-chat is boring. Recently I talked to two computer programmers who have Asperger's Syndrome. One of them told me, "I am happy because I am with my people at the computer company."

Mentors, and How to Find Them

A mentor can mean the difference between a successful and satisfying life and one in which a person becomes a loner, remaining on the fringes of society and feeling miserable. And finding a mentor can work two ways: The mentor can find the student, or the student finds the mentor. Mr. Carlock recognized my talents in science. Teachers should develop such talents, and the child should be given opportunities to exhibit them.

After college I found mentors in the cattle industry who recognized my talents. My portfolio of architectural drawings impressed them. I recommend strongly that young people make portfolios of their work. Because of poor social skills, an Asperger's person has to sell his or her work, not rely on personality!

You never know where you might find a mentor. Tom Rohrer, manager of the Swift packing plant, was the person who mentored me in the meat industry. And the door that can open the way to a mentor can be in unexpected places. I met the wife of Swift's insurance agent. My hand-embroidered western shirt impressed her, and she saw my talent in it. Good contacts resulted from that. A mentor could be your next-door neighbor who works for the telephone company and could be a guide in computer programming. Or it might be your church choir director who could help a student with musical talent.

The local community college is a resource that should be made available to high school students gifted in specific areas. I am amazed at the vast array of fascinating careers taught at these colleges. A single course taken in a community college could open many doors for students with Asperger's. Courses in these colleges range from computer programming to gardening, and many of the teachers are retired professionals who have had excellent careers. Often they still have the connections that can open many career doors!

Developing innate talent requires time and effort. I spent three years visiting every cattle feedlot in Arizona in order to learn how to design cattle-handling facilities.

Talent is like a plant. It must be nurtured carefully in order to help it grow. Many books are available from which students can teach themselves. Vast arrays of books for learning every type of computer programming, for example, are on display in large bookstores. A special responsibility falls upon teachers and mentors for directing talent into areas that can provide careers. For example, an interest in medieval history does not make a person employable, but if that history is combined with library science, the person may become eligible to work as a reference librarian.

Because of my test scores I turned to a career that had a low barrier of entry. I could not pass tests to enter medical school, but there are many other fields where there is no entry barrier. The computer industry is an easy one to enter—if one has the talent.

An older person on the Asperger's/autism spectrum can also develop his or her talent. I was in my late twenties when I learned architectural drafting. Although artistic talent showed up when I was young, my learning the special skills and requirements of mechanical drawing came later in life. I had to work very hard to be the very best at my skill in order to make up for my social deficits. To do so requires *motivation and effort.*

All the famous achievers Norm Ledgin has written about—people with a wide variety of Asperger's traits—were self-motivated and invested their best efforts in skills giving them great satisfaction. This book should add to the self-esteem of many young people with similar traits who need to know that they, too, can make a bright and happy future for themselves.

Those persons whom nature hath endowed with genius and virtue should be rendered by liberal education worthy to receive, and able to guard, the sacred deposit of the rights and liberties of their fellow citizens, and...they should be called to that charge without regard to wealth, birth or other accidental condition....

Thomas Jefferson

Hope is the thing with feathers
That perches in the soul,
And sings the tune without the words,
And never stops at all.

Emily Dickinson

Chapter One

A Challenge for Parents, Teachers, and Health-Care Professionals

Jack Herriman, conductor of the Kansas City Youth Symphony in the late 1960s and on into the 1970s, was a light-haired, slender, animated man both on and off the podium, and his methods raised eyebrows. For the repertoire of his musicians, ages twelve through twenty, Jack often selected the most daunting orchestrations. He challenged the young players with music that conductors of professional orchestras might approach cautiously.

"What on earth are you doing!" I asked Herriman. As a faintly knowledgeable parent of an orchestra member and serving on the Youth Symphony board, I was certain I understood clearly our youngsters' limitations. "This piece," I whined, "is far beyond their abilities!"

Smoothing back unruly locks like wings of Mercury, seeming ready to dash over me, Jack squinted toward a far place and snorted loudly. "I want them to *reach*, I want them

1

to *stretch*, I want them to *grow!*" His right hand flew forward like a sword thrust, menacing my ear. Then with a reassuring grin and fixing me squarely in the eyes he added gently, "They can do it, Norm, and they can do it well."

And they always did. In the summer of '69 in London the doubting BBC music director who had booked our eighty-five Kansas City youngsters on my personal plea turned to me in the first strains of rehearsal. Under Herriman's baton the children and teens were trumpeting, bowing, fluting, and kettle-drumming fervently the fiercely demanding "Overture" to *Candide* by Leonard Bernstein. The raised-eyebrows, open-mouthed BBC official nodded in awe. The orchestra was meeting, perhaps exceeding, adult standards for musicianship.

Serious Misjudgments

The experience proved my capability for serious misjudgments about achievement levels to which young people may rise when given the chance. Clearly, Jack Herriman was on the right track.

What seems a lifetime later, and having a teenaged son who is diagnosed with Asperger's Syndrome, I not only support allowing conscientious youngsters freer rein to show what they can do, I advocate it with all my heart. We parents have a tendency to sit on them, at times in the name of safeguarding them against failure, disappointment, or humiliation. Where creative effort or intensely focused interests are involved, we should stop doing that.

What exactly worries us as parents, teachers, or caregivers of children with Asperger's? Is it their vulnerability to ridicule by peers? Is it the prospect of their misreading classroom instructors? We neurotypicals see as maddening their literalness, their perseveration, or going on and on like a broken record, and their uncommon ways of reasoning. We often mistake their responses for "arguing," or perhaps "defiance."

When they are stuck on studying technical auto manuals, does it worry us that no president of the United States or successful neurosurgeon has ever found inspiration in comparing wheelbases, in probing mysteries of rack-and-pinion steering? Do we make feeble and futile efforts to redirect Asperger's youngsters toward literature that they have already found too abstract to enjoy?

An important lesson parents and other advisers of such children must learn is this: Trust them. It is time, really. After all, they have been trusting us all their lives.

Let Them Choose

Every person has the right to make his or her own mistakes. That is, in my opinion, a universal truth, but one that is not universally accepted. Most parents enjoy rehashing their experiences, so they will say to the young, "Now listen to this, and maybe you will benefit from my mistakes. What I'm about to tell you may save you a great deal of pain...."

Does anyone truly believe youngsters prefer experience-based lecturing over the prospect of personally tasting and testing life's adventures? After they respond politely with, "Thanks Mom, Dad, for the advice," does anyone believe they will not go out and take the risks their parents warned against?

Simply because Asperger's youngsters seem to own an innate sense of right and wrong, and because they are truthful and respect rules of authority, that does not mean the "kid" inside them has gotten up and left. Nature endowed our young—those with Asperger's and those without—with genes of explorers. Look away a few seconds in aisle three of a supermarket, and before you turn back, someone is paging you to pick up the little guy or the precious sweetheart near aisle twelve. Because teens are with us even less, their hideaways are more remote.

In a perfect world every youngster will select the college major, career, and spouse that parents deep down wish for. Please send me directions for finding that world.

In the case of young people with Asperger's Syndrome, as opposed to those who are neurotypical, their right to freedom and to the correct timing and parceling of more and more freedom require well-considered judgments. Those issues need special attention and deep soul-searching. We may be inclined to hold Asperger's youngsters in "protective custody" too closely, perhaps for too long. In ways of the world, we regard them as woefully naïve and terribly vulnerable.

Admittedly, with these youngsters the effort might require more cautious preparation for independence than with other children. Be patient. But also be frank, realistic, and absolutely honest, never promising the world to be an idyllic rose garden, never pledging you will be around forever to help them when they stumble. They will find their footing again. They will continue to "reach, stretch, and grow"—on their own.

They Are Always Watching

Let us look at ourselves a moment—we grown-ups who have lived through so many ups and downs, even before Asperger's children came into our lives. By and large we have a reasonably good appreciation of who and what we are. We can balance a checkbook. (I am among a few exceptions.) We do our best in career opportunities. (I know a few exceptions to that, too. I, at least, can explain my failures.)

We learn that success is not necessarily measured by how much we earn but by the satisfaction we derive from our work. (That is exactly the sort of idealism that restricts a person's earning power, take my word.) And when it comes to making our environment, our world, a better and safer place, we pride ourselves in having done our utmost. (I prefer we forgo credit in that or we could be obliged to accept blame as well.)

While there are many levels on which we *can* be credible role models, Asperger's young people will measure their combined uneasiness and idealism against our neurotypical ease of social adjustment. They will try to understand the clashing conventional values that may have driven us into work that was not our first preference. They will observe and wonder about our daily compromises. They will not always like what they see, but they *will* try to understand.

At best they may think it a pity we did not follow all the dreams we confessed burned inside us when we were their age. At worst they may conclude too many of us displaced what we call our souls (perhaps an obscure concept for them) with a passion for what is in our wallets (a tangible item whose relationship to life's natural joys is even less clear to them).

Setting Examples

In our day-to-day conduct we can certainly set examples for behavior, positive and negative. Our children note our good and bad attributes and will often use us as role models. However, I think nearly all of us do fairly well, whether parents, grandparents, teachers, school administrators, counselors, psychologists, nurses, pediatricians, therapists, and others with whom our Asperger's children come in fairly regular contact.

Asperger's youngsters assume their parents were not plagued by social liabilities that these young people now find terribly inhibiting in themselves.

People with Asperger's notice how easily we read others nonverbally, make small talk, gesture automatically, touch one another familiarly—often with special meaning. Although they might learn to do some of that, they do not quite "get it" completely. When their expressions seem eternally fixed, their sense of having been left out in such instances is apparent, at least to me. I may not feel their pain, but I sense their discomfort.

Occasionally I catch myself during conversations in which high-functioning autistic people are either participants or witnesses. I do not always keep up my guard successfully against figures of speech that the supremely literal, detailed, and logical Asperger's thinkers find strange. More than anyone outside my family, the autistic Dr. Temple Grandin, in her writings and in our conversations, has given me insight into the precise and no-nonsense ways Asperger's people think, even as they try to process the gibberish of social exchange.

Incidentally, the media have helped make a national celebrity of Temple Grandin—a living role model. She has revolutionized the cattle industry by her original designs for stock-handling facilities. As an author and lecturer, Temple has appeared repeatedly on national television. She has been featured in countless articles showing that people who have high-functioning autism can be brilliantly productive.

Yes, there are differences between the way neurotypicals behave socially and the way Asperger's or high-functioning autistics do, even with practice in processing social niceties. Primarily because of such differences, Asperger's young people want to know how others like themselves fared in this world that includes so many pretenders, exaggerators, fudgers, compromisers—even hypocrites.

Were there others with Asperger's traits who were successful in spite of their condition—perhaps *because* of their condition? Might such people serve as role models of "success," not measured as the rest of us define success but as Asperger's youngsters might define it—succeeding at great new things in a field that fascinates and captivates them.

Chapter Two

The Lonely Perspective of the Asperger's Child

A strong sense of justice pervades the thinking of a majority of Asperger's people. As a high school freshman, my son Fred tired of other boys tossing ketchup packets at him while he sat in the lunchroom. One day, as his worst tormenter sat eating and enjoying self-presumed superiority, Fred contemplated what to do with a plate of fries in front of him. He opened packet after packet of ketchup, covered the fries with the ketchup, approached the offending student, and pitched the ketchup-soaked fries onto the startled boy's shirt.

Fred said his receiving a detention was a small price to pay for getting justice, which he was confident he would never receive any other way in that public high school.

Halfway into his sophomore year, Fred passed a General Educational Development exam and was out of there and in a place designed for learning—the local community college. No one at that college throws ketchup packets at anyone else.

I share this because the reader should try to imagine what goes through an Asperger's teen's mind when he or she is being taunted for being different. It is a major "bummer." There is little or nothing the youngster can do to change himself or herself—and really, by what obligation need he or she try?

Stuck with being different, the teenager wonders whether any and all interaction with others is going to be like this through life. Then, there are the questions of "Why?" "What did I do to deserve this?" "What's wrong with me that makes me different?" "Will I ever 'get better' and fit in?"

"Even if I *am* different, did I ever do anything to those harassing and making fun of me?" "Where will all this lead?" "Are they going to get me alone and try to beat me up?" "Will they gang up and break my eyeglasses, my teeth, my ribs, my fingers, or disfigure me in some way?" "Can I muster the courage and the controlled anger to fight back successfully?"

Reasonable Questions

"School officials are standing right here watching everything without doing anything about it, so does anyone really care?" "Should I tell my parents and risk a confrontation here at school that could make this situation worse than it already is?" "I've been to one funeral of a middle school friend, so how long should I put up with this before I kill myself and have everyone weep at mine?"

These are reasonable questions under the circumstances, but the circumstances are unreasonable. Even more unreasonable is believing the circumstances in middle or secondary school, public or private, will ever change—*unless parents of children with disabilities join forces and make their outrage clear!*

Parents especially must commit themselves to greater connection with their Asperger's teenagers or pre-teens so they can detect signs of despair. They must create conditions for trust and truth that will prompt the youngsters to open up. They must reassure their tormented offspring, creating the kind of bond in which the young person will accept their active advocacy and support without fear of reprisal.

Then, of course, committed parents must follow up promises with action. They must do that regardless whether their voices break, their hands shake, or their hearts flutter while making requests or demands of school personnel.

Navigating the Maze

Not all school people are too busy to care about the discomforts of special-needs pupils. If all goes reasonably, the direct approach at the first levels of responsibility—the teacher, counselor, vice-principal, or principal—should bring relief. My experience in advocating for Fred in at least four schools, however, was that none of that worked. There were many furrowed brows followed by promises and toothy smiles, and there were sympathetic nods, but never was there any change as a result of the direct approach.

The trick, then, is for the parent to become better acquainted with the chain of accountability in the school's system. Dad or Mom must try to capture the attention of the highest-ranking administrator or even board member whose soul seems intact. If that official asks why the parent did not stay with trying others lower on the chain, the moment is ripe for reminder that the youngster's need is too urgent for the parent/advocate *not* to go—right now—where the buck stops. *That* should stir change.

When advocating for a child in a firm and informed manner, there are rules of engagement one should follow. But after being stonewalled at the child's expense, the parent must convert the approach from frustration to steady calm, maintain the family's dignity and the child's inviolability, yet turn up the intensity of the rescue mission. The stakes are too high for families of beleaguered Asperger's youngsters to behave like sheep. They must give this everything they have.

Lonely Hearts

Whether or not Asperger's people appear to prefer solitude, they value friendships. They want friends, they need friends, they deserve friends, but they have a great deal of trouble knowing how to make and keep friends.

Friends can validate the individuality and uniqueness of an Asperger's youngster by appreciating his or her creations objectively. Parents will always say, "Good job!" even if the effort should be hidden in a closet. Or, parents have been

The Lonely Perspective of the Asperger's Child

known to say, "Yeah, nice!" without ever having looked at it. Friends will likely be more honest.

Furthermore, recognizing his or her limitations in social niceties, an Asperger's young person will imitate the reciprocal social graces a peer might bring to the relationship. Parents can only coach in such matters. Friends will make and expect real responses.

As is true of many people, Asperger's youngsters will often build a shell around their innermost thoughts—their desires, fears, and imagination. The harder the effort by a parent to pierce that shell, however, the tighter a resolute youngster will become, especially one with Asperger's.

What's a Friend For?

With a friend, though, the rules change. A true friend is for telling and keeping secrets, sharing candid observations about the outside world—about *anything!* That way a frank and previously undisclosed point of view—a secret—is out and moving around in someone else's brain. Children want very much to learn to trust, and finding a reliable confidant in a peer is a classic first step.

Now comes the hard part. How do you find such a friend? Just as difficult for someone quirky, once you find him or her, how do you keep such a friend?

My inclination is to suggest, "Find a quirky friend who also needs a quirky friend!" Yet the process is not that simple.

13

Chum after chum will pass through the revolving door of Asperger's friendships and very possibly seek escape. He or she might flee at the first sign of perseveration—an Asperger's boy or girl's going on endlessly with a single point. Or there will be a glance at the door when the Asperger's youngster errs by taking something literally that was not meant that way. The first sign of an Asperger's youngster's irritation over an observed imperfection could place a new friendship at risk.

Young people might be quick to confess such a condition as, "I've got an allergy," and are ready to talk about that in brief. But few who have been diagnosed with Asperger's will say, "I've got Asperger's Syndrome." Why won't they? Because the misunderstood concept of "autism" would soon come into play. As a spectrum condition, that is difficult to clarify. Also it is a huge challenge to travel a twisted road and tell precisely how Asperger's is a *high-functioning* form of autism. Those who have Asperger's are not always articulate about describing their complicated condition.

Few with Asperger's who make the effort to explain will elaborate upon the strong significance of "spectrum disorder." Even fewer will be able to describe the uniqueness of every Asperger's person's having his or her own set of traits. Close friends need to know such things if only to brace for idiosyncrasies that are yet to crop up in the relationship—or to understand why people with the condition appear to have as many differences among them as they have similarities.

Role-Playing with Role Models

This book is not a primer on making or keeping friendships. As something of a loner myself, I am probably an unreliable authority on that. But in the context of my theme I can offer possible scenarios involving relatively bright youngsters:

Asperger's Youngster: "Have you ever heard of Gregor Mendel?"

Neurotypical New Chum: "Sure! 'Father of genetics'—a monk, right?"

AY: "Right. People say I'm like him. I have a condition he probably had."

NNC: "I know you're good at biology, all focused like you're in another world. But you're getting C's. I don't understand that. And what condition are you talking about?"

AY: "I don't test well. I take my own shorthand of concepts into the test room. I've got Asperger's Syndrome."

NNC: "Well, I don't know, you seem completely normal to me. And you're smart enough to pick up the pattern the teacher expects. Just do that!"

AY: "It's not that easy. Instead of answering questions, my head carries on arguments with them. I'm very literal, very impatient with ambiguities. By the time I respond, I don't write the answers the science teacher wants. Instead I scribble something irrelevant and figure I'd better move on."

15

NNC: "What will your grades do to your scholarship prospects?"

AY: "Mess 'em up. Maybe you can help me get past the mind blockers."

NNC: "Don't argue with questions for not liking the way they're written. Just write the answers you think they want! That's what I do, and I'm no genius. But I do get mostly A's, and I know you can, too!"

AY: "That'd be cool."

Discussing a person plucked from history—a person who had similar autistic or Asperger's traits or experiences—could open paths to friendship with peers who have common interests. That is part of what this book is about—releasing the mystique of high-functioning autism or Asperger's Syndrome from closets or lockers, giving young people with the condition someone to identify with openly.

Reference Points

General identity with known figures who had Asperger's traits can be a valuable reference point for those with the condition. Dr. Temple Grandin used a few examples in her book, *Thinking in Pictures—and Other Reports from My Life with Autism* (1995). Dr. Tony Attwood makes such references in his presentations. They know the value that such constructive name-dropping brings to broader understanding.

Continuing with role-playing such as that above, here is another possibility. Please excuse my being out of the loop about how teens actually converse at their level:

Neurotypical New Chum: "Where'd you learn to play piano like that? Do you practice—like—seven hours a day?"

Asperger's Youngster: "I hate to practice. My teacher says I'm a natural, that playing comes to me easily. Same as it did with Oscar Levant—you know, the pianist who glorified Gershwin—and the same with Mozart. Levant's mom used to tie him to the piano bench to practice, even though he didn't really need to."

NNC: "I know a little about Mozart. And I think I saw that Levant guy in a video my folks were watching, from ancient times. So what do they say, you have a gift like Mozart's?"

AY: "Maybe a gift, along with some problems. I'm like him in a few ways. I hear and see the music clearly in my mind before I even sit down to play it."

NNC: "Way cool! Is that what you mean by Asperger's?"

AY: "Pretty much, yeah. It shows up in some with Asperger's."

NNC: "Keep playing piano like that, and you'll need an agent! Can I be your agent?"

AY: "More than that, I could really use a friend."

I am not so naïve as to believe these conversations will ever take place in the forms scripted here. But my faith in this role-model topic is firm enough for me to believe similar conversations are possible.

At the very least these are examples of what young people *might* discuss about their Asperger's condition. They need such reference points as these—facts about real achievers of the past— from fields that people with such traits seem to gravitate toward.

One result of my searching biographies of famous geniuses has been confirmation that Asperger's traits may have actually contributed to their success. When we move into the area of fixations, it will become apparent that youngsters' overfocusing on a topic in which we are not interested can be of greater benefit than annoyance.

Fixations might lead to careers, to accomplishments by some beyond the expectations of a generally unimaginative society. Who would have thought that Charles Darwin's boyhood fascination with bug-collecting would tell us about our oneness with all life, wherever it exists?

Chapter Three

Dealing with Fixations that Drive Us Nuts

When you watch a small child stare at a bowl of jellybeans and notice he or she hardly blinks, you are observing a short-term fixation. When you see someone concentrating on a book or a project and you cannot get a rise out of him or her, you are dealing with a person temporarily obsessed.

With Asperger's Syndrome, fixations should be thought of as similar but more intense, deeper, and longer-lasting. Furthermore, they call into play an active commitment to the fixated object of focus by the person fixating. Usually he or she will be somewhat "hands-on" with it, make the topic an important part of his or her life at an early age, may assemble a scrapbook relating to it, possibly collect items associated with it, pull book after book off library shelves to consume every detail of the topic.

In other words, the object of focus may guide a portion of the Asperger's person's day-to-day activity, may engage him or her for quite some time, and may be dominantly present regardless what else is going on during interaction with other people. The fixation may capture the exclusive attention of an Asperger's person in such a way as to betray a lack of concern for anything else occurring at the moment.

What kinds of fixations may absorb an Asperger's youngster so completely? I met a young man with Asperger's whose knowledge of major league baseball statistics is phenomenal. Another can remember bathroom fixtures from every bathroom he has ever visited. A boy in California knows every tree that grows in every state. They often enjoy "topics such as transport (especially trains and trucks), dinosaurs, electronics and science," Dr. Tony Attwood writes in *Asperger's Syndrome: A Guide for Parents and Professionals* (1998). The "encyclopaedic knowledge" relies on detail and shows "fascination with statistics, order and symmetry."

The obsession may seem to come and go, apparently ignored for a brief period and then, suddenly, returning to front and center. Rest assured, it has been running around inside the Asperger's individual's brain, regardless whether the topic was pulled out repeatedly or seemed to vanish.

Until the Asperger's person decides otherwise, a particular fixation will rise again, inexorably, like mushrooms in a lush place on your lawn—precisely where you do not want to see mushrooms. Moreover, that will be a pattern for months, years, perhaps a lifetime.

Less likely but possible, if the fixated person has had enough of the topic, then he or she will dismiss it forever as a talking point while its lessons remain available for recall.

A fixation may even evolve into something that appears far removed from what it started out to be, as I will illustrate shortly from personal knowledge.

A Hallmark

My theme in this book tends to treat fixations kindly. While not all Asperger's people share all traits on the Asperger's continuum, obsessions are quite common among people with the condition, common enough that perhaps it should stand alone as one of the bases for diagnosis.

The fact that obsession is a hallmark feature of the Asperger's condition is both a good phenomenon and a bad one. The bad part is that, as a parent trying to understand what makes your Asperger's youngster tick and trying to be helpful, you are at a disadvantage not suffered by objective teachers or clinicians. Your child's droning on over something in which you have no interest can be excruciating and lead you to wonder what the future holds.

The good part is this: If the overfocused young person seizes upon that topic and eventually wrings everything out of it, decides to become innovative about it, and presents an original synthesis of the lessons it offers, we may all be richer for that.

Orson Welles, the actor/director, did precisely that. As a schoolboy his insistence upon arranging and overseeing dramatic productions was a way of life his teachers seemed pleased to tolerate and even encourage. The practice by the boy continued unabated into adulthood. By the time Welles was twenty-five he gave the world *Citizen Kane,* to many critics the best piece of cinematic art ever created.

Intense Preoccupation

The *Diagnostic and Statistical Manual of Mental Disorders, Fourth Edition,* published by the American Psychiatric Association in 1994 (DSM-IV) and undergoing revision as I write this, uses neither the word "fixation" on this point nor "obsession." However, the meaning of this particular criterion is clear—moreso than several others—when one realizes its framers have emphasized such concepts as "encompassing preoccupation" with any interests that are restricted in scope.

As though to make certain that diagnosticians are not dealing with passing fancies, the DSM-IV advises them to determine whether the interest is also abnormal in the intensity with which the person under study focuses upon that interest—a judgment call, yet a basis for reasonable measurement nonetheless.

Incidentally, a text revision of the DSM-IV in 2000 does not alter the criteria for Asperger's. There are new observations about the way in which older Asperger's people may handle friendships, but all the keys published in 1994 are still in place.

All the famous persons I selected for this book had tendencies to fixate in ways that were apparently abnormal. In some instances the fixations governed their career choices. For others an early chosen interest of intense focusing faded, or it shifted, and a stronger fixation supplanted it. Usually, however, a fixation of long duration had a positive bearing on their lives, but not always, as we will recognize in an account of Paul Robeson.

Long before I knew my son Fred had Asperger's, I felt as though he had placed me under siege. I was obliged to listen to a relentless outpouring of trivia. Little Freddie would come at me several times daily with facts and questions about air vents, heat registers, electrical outlets, light fixtures, fans, and cable connections. Soon he would be observing and discussing closets, bathrooms, the arrangement of hallways, stairways, windows, doors, and rooms in relation to the whole.

When entering other people's homes, Fred would ask permission to look around, even requesting to be allowed upstairs in the bedroom areas. At age five your kid is supposed to be asking you to play catch with him, not immersing himself in the smallest details of interior home design.

Fixation Expands

Did that ever let up? Not for some time. Soon the fixation expanded to freehand drawings of front elevations of homes, then floor plans tying in exactly with the elevations. I found those plans more interesting than Fred's earlier chatter about details, all of which details, by the way, made their way into his drawings. I even showed off some of his work. If his floor plans were not thoroughly functional by his judgment, Fred would throw them away and start over. I now figured the endless outpourings of questions and jabber that had preceded the drawings constituted a period of necessary observation, study, and research. At age seven or eight he was moving on rapidly.

Over the next few years and into his teens, the residential buildings grew and evolved into apartment houses, motels, small shopping centers, and then great ones. Here I must interject an interesting question: Can sideline or tangential fixations arise? Apparently yes, for he became—and continues to be—an authority on motels, having also pored intently over motel chain directories.

Next in Fred's designs came whole neighborhoods, then small and later medium-sized cities. He added residential and collector streets, major arteries, highways. The study of passenger car features in dealers' promotional literature became yet another enduring sideline. In drawing he plunged into detailing highway interchanges, complete with on-off ramps and proper striping and signing to direct motorists. He tackled the *Manual on Uniform Traffic Control Devices* and, from what I have been able to determine, found it convenient to memorize it.

While riding with me in my van, Fred often made mental notes of traffic flow problems. When we returned home he would solve the problems on paper, all with sufficient lane striping, markings, signing, and traffic signals. And the traffic lights were not just single red/amber/green signals but were always proper arrays of signal units aimed in all directions for multiple-laned traffic and, unlike what he had observed at the site, always meeting uniform standards.

No blank space on a map was safe against Fred's inventing a city to go there, a place as liveable as anyone might wish. He would name it and name every street it contained. In his conceptualizing he was making room for people who wanted to be here, in this country, and who by his view were entitled to opportunities to enjoy the living standards he enjoyed.

When he was ready for high school, Fred put away his pencils, pens, and markers and rolled up his drawings. Now he limits his designs to solving particularly sticky traffic problems, in an on-demand or as-necessary way. None of his several years' efforts were the usual computer challenge of *Sim City* creations. All designs were original, independently conceived, and the result of precise planning, building by building, street by street.

At this writing, Fred has just recently turned eighteen, is nearly halfway through college, and has entered new phases of creativity composing music and authoring well-reasoned essays. Several career possibilities lie ahead.

What Do Authorities Say?

Brenda Smith Myles and Richard L. Simpson, in their 1998 work, *Asperger Syndrome: A Guide for Educators and Parents*, discuss what they observe to be two types of obsessions: primary and secondary. In relation to the primary, the Asperger's child has "an all-encompassing level of interest in a particular topic," discussion of which "can escalate to almost tantrum-like behavior." They cite changes in speech as well as in nonverbal behavior, indicating a degree of irrationality arising from the child's attempt to share the fixation.

Secondary obsessions are those in which the child remains "lucid, focused, and ready to learn." Not only may teachers use these interests to motivate, but such obsessions may "develop into career interests."

Dr. Temple Grandin in *Thinking in Pictures* cautions against attempting to "stamp out the fixation." She sees great utility in fixations, urging teachers to channel them in order to bolster other learning. She gives a student's interest in boats as an example. A reading emphasis on boats and even doing math problems on boat speed may turn the fixation into "great motivation." She also notes that career opportunities may arise from fixations.

Dr. Grandin sees fixations as a "way to achieve some social life and friends." She cites Dr. Leo Kanner, the child psychiatrist of Johns Hopkins who first documented autism. Updating the relevancy of Kanner's findings, she calls attention to the value of computers and the Internet as keys to social interaction for people with Asperger's Syndrome.

By coincidence the man whose name we all use for the condition Asperger's Syndrome, the pediatrician Dr. Hans

Asperger, was trained in Vienna, as was Dr. Kanner. They arrived at their conclusions at almost the same moment, in 1943, with Dr. Asperger concentrating his attention on higher-functioning youngsters and also using references to "autism." They never had occasion to share their independent findings, and they never met.

Just Another Impairment?

Early on, fixations were lumped with other "abnormalities" or "impairments" in studies of high-functioning autistic children that appear in *Autism and Asperger Syndrome* (1991), edited by Uta Frith. Among attempts to determine origins and the significance of obsessions were studies that Dr. Lorna Wing led or in which she participated. With other pioneering scientists she serves the Medical Research Council in London, is author of one of the valuable papers gathered by Dr. Frith for her book, and penned the foreword in Dr. Tony Attwood's popular book, *Asperger's Syndrome.*

Dr. Attwood devotes an entire chapter to "Interests and Routines." He discusses the potential career value of such interests and also sees specialized interests as therapeutic—"a source of relaxation and enjoyment"—for young people uneasy about coping with the social side of their daily lives.

Valuable lessons about social and emotional factors such as feelings and friendships, even rules of behavior, could arise from fixations. Dr. Attwood gives the example of interest in Data, the *Star Trek* android, among people he encounters in his clinical practice. Data's difficulties in fathoming human characteristics provide a number of touch points and lessons, especially for those Asperger's people with "Trekkie" fixations.

Authorities such as Tony Attwood and other professionals who work with high-functioning autistics have established guideposts. It is now possible for a layman and writer to determine whether a historical figure, a significant achiever, was likely to have belonged on the autism/Asperger's continuum. The key to such study lies in valuable biographical accounts of the person's early years, particularly where there is reliable testimony by the subject person's contemporaries.

The value of such tracking is that young people with Asperger's find the comparisons uplifting. In a conversation with Fred early in 2000, Dr. Attwood asked how he reacted to my book, *Diagnosing Jefferson*. Tony brightened when my son replied, "I learned I can be successful in spite of my differences."

Chapter Four

A Ride in the Time Machine of Logic

When *Diagnosing Jefferson* first appeared, historians had difficulty with my conclusions—that the baffling idiosyncrasies they had described in their own works about Thomas Jefferson may qualify our Third President for placement on the autism/Asperger's continuum.

Historians repeatedly caution readers and students against "presentism"—confusing history and its major players with modern circumstances. I can understand that, but I found some historians unable to accept that today's science might illuminate an enigma left over from the past.

Several historians I have contacted hesitate to concede that what we know of the trait pattern for Asperger's Syndrome might raise our understanding of a puzzling historical figure. The fact that Jefferson possessed an abundance of such traits, behaving in ways exceeding minimum criteria for definitive diagnosis, is thought by skeptics to be of little relevance. Better to keep the icon and ignore whatever it was that made him so quirky and so seemingly self-contradictory. Such a mind-set is almost like believing that Moses could never have had a distracting toothache or other ailment while wandering in the desert for decades, simply because no health-ministering associate was close by to record it.

The real problem, I am confident, is the word "autism." More accurately, the problem is the *public perception* of autism. Despite efforts to raise awareness in people about a condition affecting humankind everywhere, I doubt more than one in a hundred knows autism is not always about "grossly-disabled, poorly-functioning children," as the neurologist/author Dr. Oliver Sacks laments is the prevailing impression.

"This concept needs to be expanded," Dr. Sacks wrote in support of Uta Frith's work, *Autism and Asperger Syndrome*, "for there are also children and especially adults who have good language and intellectual skills, who can sometimes, indeed, manage to pass as 'normal', and yet are still fundamentally autistic."

Causes of Autism

With such problems of acceptance as the foregoing in mind, I invite readers to travel in the Time Machine of Logic. Before launch we should share the known causes of autism. The condition results from one of three circumstances: *Either it is inherited, or it is the result of an accident during pregnancy or birth, or it results from an accident in infancy.* In the latter two circumstances, medical or environmental factors that were not present when we were cave people or tree dwellers should probably be discounted from centuries-old consideration. But what about that autistic gene? When did it spring forward, and is such a gene present in other species?

The estimate of how frequently Asperger's occurs is running fairly steadily at one in 250 births. A minor epidemic is upon us—the result either of better diagnosis or of environmental factors whose effects we underestimate, are uncertain about, or refuse to control. If we were to consider genetic possibilities alone and look back in time, we may not derive an accurate pre-Industrial Revolution incidence, but we would be reasonably safe speculating that the condition has swum freely in the human gene pool for centuries—if not millennia.

As for that word, "condition," I seized upon it as a substitute for "disorder," though occasionally I use the latter. There are so many factors on the plus side of Asperger's Syndrome, I often fail to recognize that (in the context of societal norms) these are people of seriously limited skills in critical areas. Because I tend to stand back from practicing a few of the social graces myself, I believe some worries about the social side are slightly overblown. But I will never go against anyone's efforts to improve youngsters' social skills or to alleviate legitimate concerns about them.

My positive attitude about benefits to society from the creative mind of Asperger's people drives me forward. At times

I proceed in the manner of a broken-field runner, sidestepping such judgments as "suffering from Asperger's," a phrase that makes me shudder. Except for the way we and their peers treat them, and except for their consequent sense of unease, in what way are Asperger's people suffering?

Impairment as a Benefit?

I have the same problem with the word "impairment." This value-based word covers behavior that runs off the conventional track. If I were to oppose, philosophically, and speak forcefully against a few of the more selfish practices sustaining professional sports, even as I participate occasionally as a cheering spectator, would my complaint render me apparently "impaired" in the eyes of others? Yes, and it might also make me seem a hypocrite.

In my earlier work I cited the Declaration of Independence as an example of Jefferson's "impairment" because a portion of his background argument for liberty was flawed. But let me put forward a couple of questions in general terms: What if, as a result, impairment does not occur for society? What if social gain is the consequence instead? Does the duck that we refer to as "impairment" still look like and walk like a duck, or has it somehow taken on the grace of a swan?

Resuming our ride in the Time Machine of Logic, the arguments Temple Grandin makes for unexpectedly beneficial results of so-called impairment are compelling. She has written in various ways that *"genius is an abnormality,"* an observation worth everyone's deep and honest consideration. I will give that concept further treatment later in this book.

Temple writes:

> Civilization would probably pay a terrible price if the genes that cause autism and Asperger's Syndrome were eradicated. The world might become a place full of highly social yakkity-yaks who would never do anything new or creative.

That brings us back to the nagging question that tends to place me at odds with historians: Has it not always been this way? Is it not reasonable to assume Asperger's Syndrome—in some unnamed form—has affected people possibly from the start of human existence? Is it not also reasonable to speculate that the condition may have visited other life forms in the evolutionary ladder? What we now know of common developmental triggers—in the DNA of humans and that of other species—lets us reason that the condition we have named Asperger's may have a longer history than anyone has ever imagined.

The underappreciated history of Asperger's is potentially more interesting because of variability. No two individuals with Asperger's Syndrome have exactly the same set of traits. Adding to our fascination, think of the *spectrum* dimension of autism. Autism's neurological basis yields a virtual rainbow of variously needful, always special individuals.

Chapter Five

Finding and Offering Relevant Role Models

Does my living with an Asperger's teenager give me an advantage for spotting people in history who may have had the same condition? Yes, I benefit from residing in a home clinic of sorts. Every day I face such issues as literalness, routinization, perhaps too strict an adherence to rules, a surprising use of advanced logic, a dogged pursuit of details, a hammering away at fixations, and a few uncommon perspectives of humor or of pathos.

"Ah-*ha!*" I might proclaim in this setting, "I remember a film clip of Paul Robeson's going on about a small musical point, doing that same kind of perseverating." So I am off for another peek at one of the persons I identified for this work.

I have told a number of people what I am working on in behalf of bolstering youngsters' self-esteem. Several have suggested celebrities present and past for me to study. I have explored all of those suggestions and have rejected most of their proposed prospects for lacking suitable matches with diagnostic criteria. Because objective biographical material is sparse for contemporary celebrities, I have distanced myself from considering living subjects. I do not want the all-too-common misperception of autism to put me in contention with them.

Anyone who reads history or biographies may find clues about other persons who had Asperger's traits, perhaps in abundance. Whether those figures will fit an Asperger's matrix is another matter. For that determination I rely heavily, but not entirely, on the previously mentioned *Diagnostic and Statistical Manual.* Arguments persist over some features that the DSM-IV includes and over a few that it omits. Sensory issues have not yet found their way into the list of criteria for Asperger's, for example. By and large, however, the American Psychiatric Association is accepted in the United States as the authority on the subject. The DSM-IV is the "bible" here for professional diagnosis.

The Diagnostic Criteria

What does the DSM-IV say about the "Asperger's Disorder," which made its way into the book for the first time in the 1994 edition? Without my repeating the entire standard here, parts of which seem open to interpretation, I will sum its main points. I base my searches on this DSM-IV standard closely, but I do not follow a strict orthodoxy.

On the interactive side diagnosticians look for at least two of the following four:

- *An observable disability in nonverbal behavior*

- *Failures in peer relationships*

- *A lack of positive sharing*

- *Relative numbness in social or emotional relationships*

In terms of behavioral characteristics that do not rely on interaction, diagnosticians look for only one of these four:

- *Fixations or conspicuous overfocusing*

- *Nonfunctional routines*

- *Odd motor mannerisms*

- *Persistent attachment to parts of objects*

These criteria, even in their longer and equally ambiguous forms, are generally understandable to clinicians who diagnose professionally. But this is not rocket science. It is observational diagnosis. Some references may seem strange to us laymen, such as the last item about parts of objects. Would a rickety folding chair that apparently came from a bridge set, for example, qualify as part of an object? If so, that criterion is a match for the Canadian pianist Glenn Gould, who carried such a chair everywhere, used it in every performance, and eventually wore the seat clear through.

There are more criteria, but only one is thought by Asperger's authorities to be relevant. The important one is this:

A clinically-judged impairment of a social, work, or "other" important activity as a result of the "disturbance."

Remember, please, there is a bias among neurotypicals, and such words as "impairment" and "disturbance" are rooted in that bias—that view of what is either "normal" or "abnormal." We are all forced, however, to take into major account the professional definitions of this condition, no matter how harsh they may seem to some of us. We are stuck with those negative references no matter how offensive they may be to people with Asperger's Syndrome, many of whom never think of themselves as abnormal to the slightest degree.

All told, then, the candidate for a diagnosis of Asperger's Syndrome should meet at least four criteria—perhaps *must* meet— when diagnosticians use the DSM-IV as their strict standard.

The criteria appearing in the DSM-IV that we may get away with *not* counting are "late-onset" items. These are factors that are not seen in individuals as children who are diagnosed with Asperger's at an older age. Essentially these represent *no childhood delay* in areas such as language skills, cognitive development, age-appropriate self-help, and curiosity about surroundings.

Dr. Attwood has said these last items do not belong. I agree because they seem more suited to judgments about the presence of Kanner's autism than of Asperger's.

Continuum of Traits

In my book about Thomas Jefferson I introduced a continuum of more than 100 traits associated with Asperger's. I marked roughly two-thirds of them as appearing in reports about Jefferson, given largely by his contemporaries. About fifty of those that I marked were supported by considerable evidence. Another seventeen were strongly suspected of Jefferson because of significant references in biographies. I based that list of traits on several models from sources around the world.

Once a layman such as myself becomes acquainted with commonly observed Asperger's behavioral traits, it is not a far reach to recognize them when they emerge in biographies. They are like clues a detective might track.

In reading biographies of people I suspected were on the autism/Asperger's continuum, I paid closest attention to their behavior as children and as young adults.

When persons with the condition reach teen years, they start learning adaptive behavior and will change their ways in social interaction. This is true today, and it was true in the time of, say, Darwin or Curie. I am quite certain about transformations in the behavior of Thomas Jefferson roughly halfway through his long life. In time he became perceptive about the way others saw him. In his writings he admitted as much, vowed he would change, and evidently did.

I caution the reader against exclaiming, "I didn't know Mozart had Asperger's!" To be honest, I did not know either and still do not know it, although I suspect it. There is no reasonable observational opportunity for a clear, confirmed diagnosis of Mozart, so long as he has reposed in a grave these past two centuries. As Dr. Temple Grandin taught me, we can only say he was "on the autism/Asperger's continuum." She is a scientist. I am not. I yield that point.

I am careful not because I am uncertain. I am careful because I want to stay credible. My credibility over Jefferson remained intact because so many Asperger's authorities judged my conclusions as sound, based on the evidence.

In considering historical role models for youngsters with Asperger's, we should keep an eye on the goal: To give young people with the developmental condition of Asperger's Syndrome examples of brilliant eccentrics who may inspire–

- Hope of success to which they may become entitled by their work and talent

- Hope of their living a full, happy life that is everyone's entitlement

- Hope of creating for us something unique and lasting, if that is the legacy they wish their special genius to represent for all eternity

Chapter Six

A Caring Statesman with a Double-Tracked Mind

Thomas Jefferson has been the most carefully studied of all presidents of the United States. He was perhaps the most complex person ever to hold that office. He was certainly the most prolific of chief executives as a writer and political philosopher. He ranged farthest in his interests, which included the natural sciences, agriculture, architecture, languages, and law.

The information that biographers and historians have passed along to us about Jefferson shows clearly that his behavior matched not just four but *five* of the required criteria for a diagnosis of Asperger's Syndrome. Much of that personal information is from Jefferson's own pen or from writings of his contemporaries. Yet, in his absence, we can only place him on the continuum and not claim a definitive diagnosis for him.

The next-born of his parents' ten children, Jefferson's sister Elizabeth, was from all descriptions a person who could be

Thomas Jefferson (1743-1826)

placed lower on the autism continuum. As noted in my earlier book, the presence of such a condition could be traced through their mother, a member of the Randolph family, and a few of her kin were famously idiosyncratic. Furthermore, testimony exists that Thomas's younger brother, Randolph Jefferson, a twin, was quite slow or at the very least persistently "childlike." Among twins the possibilities are present for neurological problems affecting only one of the pair.

An achiever of the first rank, Jefferson took greatest pride in three accomplishments that had nothing to do with his presidency—authorship of both the Declaration of Independence and the Statute of Virginia for Religious Freedom and his founding of the University of Virginia. He ordered only those three accomplishments to be inscribed on his tombstone, which bears no mention of his political service to Virginia and the United States, nor mention of the Louisiana Purchase. The huge land acquisition from France doubled the size of the nation and was his most notable achievement as president.

A Confession

Early in 2000 the Thomas Jefferson Foundation announced it had accepted conclusions of historical and scientific research that paired Jefferson with Sally Hemings, his late wife's half-sister and a house slave at Monticello. The relationship with Sally reportedly lasted thirty-eight years until his death in 1826. A Foundation spokesperson, Dianne Swann-Wright, when interviewed on NBC's *Today* program, responded to a question about Jefferson's seemingly contradictory behavior by confessing, "There was a personal side of Thomas Jefferson that many of us just simply haven't been able to understand."

The greatest difficulty in fathoming his personality for over two centuries, including his time in public service, was that observers and scholars assumed the spectacularly brilliant Jefferson was neurologically normal. He was a very kind and generous man, and he had a marvelously keen mind. But it should have been obvious from considerable evidence of his eccentricities that he was definitely not normal.

A nation's chief executive greeting dignitaries while dressed in odd, frayed clothing, worn-down bedroom slippers, his hair uncombed, at times with a pet mockingbird perched on his shoulder, was not what I would regard as normal, no matter how much I revere the man. A precise detailer who kept records of all expenditures for six decades, yet could not reconcile them to avoid going broke, was not normal. A man of science who, alone in this habit, believed he could ward off colds and flu by plunging his feet into cold water every morning for most of his life was not normal.

We are also looking at a father who loved his daughters but could not hug them, a designer/architect who took fifty-four years to build his house, and a political leader whose poor speaking skills sent second-row listeners scurrying for the next day's paper to learn what he said. Those are features of a person one would scarcely consider normal.

Guard Against Realities

In *American Sphinx: The Character of Thomas Jefferson* (1997) Joseph J. Ellis wrote that Jefferson was capable of reasoning along two tracks. What the historian referred to as "interior defenses" protected Jefferson against realities he did not want to face, such as his dependency upon slaves and his declining financial condition.

A difference in reasoning is common among Asperger's children and grownups. We recognize it when they are "either-or" about an issue and will not enter middle ground, or when they confuse the ideal and the real in conversation. I was grateful that Ellis had attempted such an analysis of our most enigmatic president at the moment I was preparing to write *Diagnosing Jefferson.*

Jefferson also had sensory problems common to people with Asperger's—an admitted hypersensitivity to the sound of voices mixing in conversation and voices raised in argument and a hyposensitivity to loud sounds in his nailery at Monticello. Dr. Hans Asperger found both hearing sensitivities to be present simultaneously in subjects of his pioneering studies. Furthermore, Jefferson required soft clothing on parts of his body—waist, hips, legs, and feet—and tight clothing across his chest for calming pressure. These are similar to the personal sensory problems of Temple Grandin.

When he broke his right wrist in 1786 in Paris, he demonstrated quickly that he was ambidextrous, an ability found among some people with Asperger's. To the extent that his body language inspired comments by observers, he was conspicuously awkward in gestures while standing to listen or speak, and awkward while seated in meetings. Because of a report by a contemporary, I believe he barely moved his arms while walking, which is a feature of gait common with Asperger's people.

A Quiet Man

Jefferson was not thought to be much of a conversationalist, John Adams having remarked on that characteristic of the young Virginian after they served in the Continental Congress. He preferred to draw back and write whatever was on his mind. He left something in the neighborhood of 20,000 letters among his writings, having duplicated most of them on a mechanical apparatus he perfected for that purpose.

By age five, Jefferson had read all the books in the library of his father, Peter, a surveyor/mapmaker. Those books would likely have been substantially technical. Historian Merrill D. Peterson has estimated Jefferson's intelligence quotient at 150.

Dr. Grandin has commented that Jefferson was a "specific-to-general" thinker, one who concluded general patterns from the various details he observed or put into play. His design for Monticello reflected that. He did not start with a rectangle and proceed to fit everything into it. Both the outer and inner designs were free-form in style, employing half-octagons in a utilitarian and highly aesthetic manner.

Dr. Grandin added that specific-to-general is the direction in which her mind works and that such a process is also true of many people with autism. Neurotypicals, on the other hand, start with generalized concepts and fit details into them. As an example, ask me to design a floor plan, and I will start with a rectangle every time.

The choice of Thomas Jefferson as a subject for study in terms of Asperger's characteristics was entirely accidental. I happened to be reading a six-volume work by Dumas Malone (*Jefferson and His Time*, 1948-81) and was simultaneously attempting to understand my son Fred's freshly diagnosed condition. That was in late 1996.

Malone tossed so many unexplained idiosyncrasies into the mix that I began to see behavioral resemblances to Fred. I wrote down the nature of those quirks, counting an impressive number of them. That has since allowed me to present Asperger's children with a role model no one had ever guessed they might look to for encouragement, assurance, and inspiration.

A number of parents have said my book has meant a great deal to them and to their Asperger's children. I am grateful for such comments because that is precisely why I went ahead with such a project—to make the point that, despite his enigmatic characteristics, Jefferson made lasting contributions to humankind.

Chapter Seven

A Cuddly Nobel Winner with a Bite

Albert Einstein, winner of the Nobel Prize in 1921 and father of the theory of relativity, increased our understanding of the fundamentals of physics. His early findings strengthened scientists' practical perceptions of motion, energy, matter, and light, enabling great gains, not only in electrodynamics, but also in space. His scientific insight proved critical to the Allies in bringing World War II to a successful conclusion.

Who was this man cited by *Time* as "the pre-eminent scientist in a century dominated by science" and named by the magazine as Person of the Century? How did so many people come to revere this apparently cuddly man who avoided the practice of running a comb through his hair? "He could be alternately warmhearted and cold; a doting father, yet aloof," according to the *Time* account. While drawn into deep concern for other people, whether friends or strangers, Einstein recoiled from intimacy.

Albert Einstein (1879-1955)

Born in Germany with a swollen and misshapen head, young Albert reportedly did not speak until he was three. His father and uncle were electrochemists. His mother loved music so passionately that it rubbed off on the child. Einstein became a "music addict" in childhood, struggling to master the violin before turning to joys of the piano.

Einstein had no friends and rarely mixed with children his age. He was, in the vernacular of the period, the "odd boy out." Even as a child he was introspective and avoided light conversation. If something caught his interest, however, he had the "concentration of a watchmaker" and a "laserlike ability to focus," according to chroniclers of his life. Like Marie Curie in the presence of her family or others, Einstein yielded to no distractions.

Alternately Sour and Amiable

In school young Einstein habitually repeated teachers' questions before replying. That was his way of meeting demands of rote learning. His manner of dealing with teachers and with other students was such that they "kept their distance." He dropped out of high school when business failures required the family to leave Germany for Italy. From there they moved to Switzerland.

The change in environment did little for his generally sour personality until he saw an opportunity to study at Zurich Polytechnic. His sister remarked that an astonishing change came over him simply from his making application. In the words of Denis Brian in *Einstein: A Life* (1996)—

> The nervous, withdrawn dreamer had become an amiable, outgoing young man with a tart sense of humor. Was it (his) escape from purgatory?

Although he seemed aglow with the happy promise of scientific study, Einstein failed his entrance examination. Special arrangements were made to let him enter, however, because of his relative youth and brilliance. Still, he lapsed and appeared to prefer self-instruction to the professors' teaching methods, cutting classes regularly.

"You're a clever fellow, Einstein," one of his professors told him, "but you have one flaw. You won't let anyone tell you a thing." Although Einstein had hoped to land a position with the school after receiving his degree, no one recommended hiring him. He moved on to work as a tutor and then took an examiner's job in the patent office in Bern.

Descriptions are common of the misplaced patent official's padding about in worn-down bedroom slippers. When we factor in the scientist's reputation for bizarre clothing choices and his unconcern about appearance, the identification with Asperger's traits is somewhat familiar. Einstein's uncombed hair was always a signature feature.

Charming—but Also Tactless

Einstein's principal problem was his lack of a tactful manner for interacting with teachers in early years and interacting with acquaintances throughout his life. Although he had a certain charisma owing to superior intelligence—even a slight charm arising from a love of punning—his overall attitude sent the wrong message. While capable of "wise and well-informed" conversation, a blatantly antagonistic style of behavior canceled the attraction.

Einstein could, and did, fall in love, but his early aversions to sentimental display surfaced and interfered with whatever happiness love might have inspired. He was also fickle. Once after falling in love, he abandoned the object of his affection to pursue another young woman. By all guarded reports and rumors, the twice-married Einstein—a husband and father espousing causes to help the human race in its pursuit of happiness—had little appreciation for ways in which family responsibilities might bring him bliss.

Does Einstein belong on the autism/Asperger's continuum? In 1999 a group of scientists studying a portion of his preserved brain concluded it was malformed in ways "possibly" enhancing his intelligence. Of course, the medical basis for autism and Asperger's Syndrome is a brain malformation that gives rise to neurological differences, but the scientific team did not venture very far down that path.

Under existing diagnostic criteria, would Einstein possibly belong on the autism/Asperger's continuum? An item raising doubt might be the late onset of speech, which the DSM-IV presents as a disqualifier. However, Dr. Tony Attwood has said that the American Psychiatric Association is dead wrong on that point.

Little has come down to us about Einstein's nonverbal behaviors. As a boy he did not play games with other children, whether from awkwardness or from simple lack of interest.

Relevant signs of fixations lie in young Albert's interest in his father's field of electrochemistry. His own early successful searches in theoretical physics notwithstanding, Albert preoccupied himself by reworking them for new outcomes that were not always credible. His violin-playing obsession must count, the more interesting side of which is that he found his affair with the instrument to be something of a struggle.

Overfocusing, then, is strongly characteristic of people on the continuum, as are emotional impairments that crop up in descriptions of Einstein. As shown earlier, however, social impairment is still a relative term about which qualitative uncertainties continue to spin, and social issues affected Einstein as well.

Others' Social Issues

Apparently John Hartford, about whom you will read later, had no problem of impairment in social matters. He could be quiet, reserved, but neither withdrawn nor showing any tendency to be a loner.

On the other hand, Jefferson—at heart a loner—overcame inhibitions by accommodating himself to social demands, knowing that he could at his choosing escape to his preferred solitude. True impairment for Jefferson surfaced in more critical areas.

Previewing how this issue impacted famous figures whom you will meet shortly: Paul Robeson handled the social (if not the emotional) side of his personality cheerfully, but he retreated to self-isolation as well. Fixations induced Robeson's impairment along with an inability to gauge the social effect of his speechifying. Despite his great artistry he lost his means of making a living.

Gregor Mendel seemed evenhanded about the social encounters in his monastic life. Charles Darwin did so as well during his continuing scholarship, in spite of torment over the clash of science and religion. Impairments of other kinds than friendships were vivid for them both. The young Wolfgang Amadeus Mozart was more troubled than successful in social interaction. His problems will be discussed in a later chapter.

Social experiences of my other selected role models ranged from moderate to spectacular impairment. With Carl Sagan and Orson Welles, for example, one seldom knew where one stood. Was it their work that made them grouchy? Was it their inability to win for their work the approval they believed it had earned?

Although Einstein won the Nobel Prize for his efforts, he appeared to need something more but never made clear what that should be. As for his social impairment, those who did not know Einstein loved and revered him; many who were close to the man did not.

Yet this quickly recognizable teddy bear celebrity, regardless of his full plate of eccentricities, remains a giant in our memory for unequaled achievements in science. Perhaps that memory is the "something more" that Einstein seemed to require.

Chapter Eight

A Self-Censoring Scientist Who Knew Too Much

Because Charles Darwin was a product of Georgian and Victorian times and because he respected Scripture, he grew conflicted by what he had learned traveling in South America and the Pacific as a young natural scientist. He was fearful of the effect his findings might have on a society that believed, with only scattered doubts, that God had created humans specially and given us dominion over all other forms of life.

As a boy and throughout his school years, Darwin had a reputation for calling attention to himself, telling tall tales, and showing disdain for formal education. This masked a lack of self-confidence and an emotional detachment from family members, especially after his mother died when he was eight years old. As was true of Jefferson and will be learned of others I will describe in this book, he could remember scarcely anything about his mother.

Charles Darwin (1809-1882)

The evidence Darwin carried home from his five-year (1831-36) scientific voyage aboard the *HMS Beagle*, therefore, was a terrible sword against prevailing and comforting religious thought, a sword wielded by someone not yet thirty years of age who had a reputation for being imprudent.

Some historians have said he spent the next twenty years "refining" his discovery before writing *On the Origin of Species*, published in 1859. More recently scholars have argued Darwin's secret so tormented him that it caused him to fall ill with stomach cramps and headaches (the same ailments afflicting Jefferson) along with over-reported bouts of diarrhea during stress. Then followed Darwin's skin disorders, rheumatoid pains, insomnia, and heart palpitations, much of which I believe could have resulted from mishandling chemicals in earlier laboratory pursuits.

One school of thought regarding his poor health has been that Darwin was hypersensitive to heat and suffered multiple allergies, that those were genetic tendencies passed along in a family plagued by obesity. The handling of laboratory chemicals, it should be pointed out, could also induce multiple allergy-like symptoms. Good evidence to the contrary—that Darwin's anxieties triggered such conditions—lay in his having grown worse the harder he applied himself to formulating the theoretical underpinnings of evolution.

Historical Persecution

The notebooks Darwin kept after returning from his voyage (and kept hidden from associates) might appear to support the refinement argument. On the other side, some of the notes he entered in them reflect fears—that his findings would be judged iconoclastic, if not the work of a heretic. In one notebook he cited "persecution of early astronomers" for their scientific discoveries, no doubt recalling the plight of Galileo. Furthermore, prevailing laws against blasphemy and sedition in evangelical England, where there is no formalized church-state separation, were realities not lost on him.

Darwin moved with deliberate slowness until other naturalists began to dance around the edges of evolutionary theory. None had devoted to natural science, however, the intensity of prolonged study that he had, nor had any suffered such strain and poor health over it. The release of *Origin* did, in fact, excite an expected socio-religious trauma, even "spin" by a philosophical school known (unfortunately and without Darwin's complicity) as "Social Darwinism." Scientific conscience and the threat of competing theories finally compelled Darwin to release his discovery.

Now where from all this, plus a few facts that I have not yet disclosed, do we find Darwin a place on the autism/Asperger's continuum?

"A man of clockwork routine" is a biographer's description, taking care of one of the necessary criteria. Ample reports of a conspicuous reserve and avoidance of peer play furnish us another, yet his gentle nature eased his establishing friendships, regardless of the fact that he chose not to join other boys on the playing fields. His tendency toward being a loner and his emotional distancing from his father and sisters provide yet another link to DSM-IV warrants. The "impairment" factor completing the match with diagnostic criteria might be seen in his waiting so long to release results of a five-years' field study and the correlations and interpretations of those findings.

Hit-and-Miss Education

Are acute apprehensions a contributor to "impairment," whether or not such fears are well-founded? I believe they are. As background, for a time Darwin's hit-and-miss educational training had included study for the ministry. He found didactic presentations hard to swallow and disliked divinity school as much as he had an earlier effort that would have pointed him toward a medical career. According to Dr. Hans Asperger, young people in his 1940s studies preferred to "follow their own ideas" rather than comply with rigid directions and demands of instructors. Following his science regardless of an inner struggle against conventional "wisdom" is exactly what Darwin believed was necessary for him to do. This led him into a prolonged self-impairment.

Darwin had inadvertently entered a conflict between the formal doctrine of the age, which was expression of faith in God and lessons of the Bible as interpreted by a state-sanctioned church, and wholly new explanations of how humans came into existence.

Further "impairment" was evident in Darwin's carrying his overfocusing into such matters as significant differences among beaks of finches and among shells of tortoises. Earlier I referred to "perseveration" as a form of talking at length about details, but the word—which a developmental psychologist first taught me as applicable to my son's repetitions—may also apply to fixations. In that sense Darwin continued alternately to fragment his studies and then weave them into a theoretical construct the world was unready to accept.

Aware of the potential impact of his findings and wavering between apprehension and courage, he worked secretly and, at last, publicly. Where I live, some 143 years after the release of *Origin,* a substantial and often dominant portion of Kansas citizens is still unready to come to terms with evolution.

A Gentle, Literary Side

What seems such a pity in this review of Darwin is that the torment wrought by his work affected such an endearing person, one biographer going so far as to offer the judgment, "his gentleness was overwhelming." He was also a very literary man, poring over poems and plays "by the hour," collecting old verses, becoming "a superb writer" in his own right.

At the age of ten he had begun collecting insects, moving on to shells, rocks, and birds' eggs. Observing him off to one side, classmates said generally that he was "old for his age...in manner and mind." Darwin's early naturalist interests and fixations were harbingers of things to come, dooming attempts by his family to direct him toward medicine or the ministry.

That a fixated Darwin actually found his career footing earlier than his own family realized is one of those lessons of history from which parents and teachers may profit. If they oversee children with a possible or known condition of Asperger's pursuing an interest that seems odd by their judgment, they should build on that interest, as Dr. Grandin has suggested, rather than try to redirect offbeat interests toward something else.

Simply to go with what such a child finds compelling and interesting may be doing civilization a great favor.

Despite the puzzles that Darwin the boy and Darwin the man represented, he made vitally significant discoveries in the search that could, one day, define more thoroughly who and what we are.

ASPERGER'S AND SELF-ESTEEM

Chapter Nine

A Showman Who Peaked Too Soon

Any story about actor/director Orson Welles, particularly about the achievements in entertainment for which we know him best, comes roughly to completion at a point only one-third through his life of seventy years. His tragedy lay in being so far ahead of his time that show business as we know it could not keep pace.

Staging dramas was more than the focus of Welles's life. It was an obsession so strong it dominated his childhood—if anyone reading about him can believe there ever was in Welles's life such a period as childhood.

When I was a boy living in Northern New Jersey I remember picking up the New York papers one morning with surprise to read of a panic Orson Welles had prompted the previous night over the radio. Listeners of a broadcast in which he had performed reacted in such fear of danger from outer

Orson Welles (1915-1985)

space that the papers carried photos of people holding weapons, ready to fight invading aliens.

Welles's 1938 dramatization of H.G. Wells's *War of the Worlds* was so realistic for that time in radio entertainment, many listeners thought the invasion was truly taking place. A medium on which we all depended heavily in those days, radio had never known the likes of such a studio drama, with its breaking-news type interruptions and believable sound effects of creepy invaders seizing or zapping citizens of New Jersey. Even as a boy I wondered: Why had those frightened people forgotten it was Halloween and that this guy was simply trying to scare the daylights out of them?

Depression Entertainment

My father, Cy Ledgin, was active in the entertainment world, so at an early age I became aware of stars brightening our lives on what we referred to then as "stage, screen, and radio." During the Great Depression show business was a diversion, the escape that many required to pull themselves through emotionally. In our family "showbiz" also meant pulling through financially. My dad taught tap-dancing to little girls whose moms wanted them recreated as clones of Shirley Temple, child actress and probably the most popular entertainer of her time. Movies and radio helped lucky survivors of the Depression like us see past those unfortunate people who stared hauntingly from their "homes" made of cardboard and tarpaper.

Welles was criticized for mixing fiction with what seemed, by his brilliant direction, an unfolding, actual event. A verdict from another perspective and from hindsight might be that Welles was simply better at what he did than any previous dramatist. Journalists described this twenty-three-year-old actor with the haunting eyes and the deeply powerful voice as a genius. They hinted broadly, however, that Orson Welles might be "touched," a euphemism short of suggesting the need for a straitjacket.

The creative actor/director soon moved on to Hollywood, where rumors flew that he would portray the publisher William Randolph Hearst in an unfavorable light. The result was *Citizen Kane*, a motion picture so new in style that many critics did not know what to make of it. Of course, audiences loved it. When critics arrived at that realization, they assessed Welles's work as arguably the best thing ever put on film.

Welles made the movie when he was only twenty-five. Released in 1941, *Citizen Kane* was the only film that was entirely Welles's creation. Although he did not yet know it, in that one effort he had reached the pinnacle of his uniquely creative career.

Radical Innovator

What do conservative societies do with such radical innovators? Figuratively, they burn the offenders at the stake. Then, upon collective reflection and after a respectable passing of years, societies that had discredited new ideas end up appropriating and absorbing them as mainstream convention.

Modern so-called docudramas owe their mass appeal to *Citizen Kane*. Artfully aimed camera shots owe their popularity, if not origin, to Welles, who tried what had worked for Sergei Eisenstein in Russia and Fritz Lang in Germany. Alfred Hitchcock also mastered such pulse-quickening camera techniques.

Welles's service in four roles—producer, director, writer, and star performer—was unusual. Few had ever done that. Only Charlie Chaplin had succeeded before Welles, also writing the musical scores. Some Chaplin works were brilliant in the comic and poignant sense, such as *City Lights*, and several were not. But no single effort during the first half-century of cinema had the "wow" effect of *Citizen Kane*.

The script was even more captivating to filmgoers than Orson's direction. Welles spun out the story as a mystery, an enigma of detail that media people and the public (as portrayed in the movie) believed had governed the psyche of the hugely successful Kane-as-Hearst. Solution of the mystery did not arrive until a few seconds before the end. It was a "your eyes only" experience for the audience, not for characters in the film plot.

Who would not love such confidentiality—a knowing wink from the Orson Welles who once tricked so many on Halloween? His deference to others in final credits cemented the audience's engagement with a one-of-a-kind showman.

Gone Tomorrow

Ah, but for Welles it would be "here today, gone tomorrow." Hollywood, by the end of the magical 1930s, was on a roll. The industry was awash in dazzling glitz. Welles's *Citizen Kane* threatened to change everything. Associates in moviemaking claimed he had "ruined Hollywood" by redirecting audiences toward a new brand of dramatic quality. As a result, except for an already-contracted movie, *The Magnificent Ambersons* (1942), no one would back Welles's complete holding of the reins in any more filmmaking ventures.

Welles tried for another twenty years without success to win financial backing that would let him produce movies on the scale of *Kane.* Producers preferred to remain with sure-fire song-and-dance fluff, or schmaltzy fare adapted from best-sellers with the mood-music volume turned up.

Some observers thought *Kane* had been a fluke. The Hollywood rich, rising past depression and war, would not take a chance on him. Shortly after his triumph, Welles's star went into rapid descent. From such memorable acting roles as those in *Jane Eyre, The Long Hot Summer,* and especially that of Harry Lime in *The Third Man,* he set aside most of his earnings for future producing, but he could never quite raise enough to approach his independent screen goals.

For all his innovative genius, chroniclers of Orson's life found him to be overtly unlikeable. As a child "he could not really play with kids." One biographer noted that friendships "never...satisfied him." He was awkward, talked too much, argued with teachers about their subjects, and tended to be pedantic and condescending.

Welles was so much a loner, "a boy without friends," "a forbidding master of solitude," that at socially structured dances he was at times found to be dancing alone. So far we are not off the pattern of others with Asperger's traits, whose biographers have described their tendencies to be loners.

Orphaned Early

Young Orson was often fixated, whether on theatrics or verse. "He knew acres of verse," and "great stretches of poetry," as contemporaries described his grasp. He was also quite musical, and could play the piano and draw very well. His mother had been a concert pianist. She died when he was eight. His father died when he was thirteen. His parents had been separated since he was six. He had a brother named Richard who was schizophrenic and committed suicide.

With relatives and mentors young Orson traveled extensively, circling the globe twice by the time he was eleven, receiving encouragement to lead theatrical productions in all the schools he attended. Early in life he learned to be quite manipulative, insisting upon his way in all things, and he reportedly built lie upon fib out of habit.

I believe writers and critics have been too broadly judgmental of Welles, whose early caretakers appeared to have turned him into a special breed of spoiled brat. They pampered and indulged him. They may have attempted to relieve Orson's despair over his orphaned status.

Furthermore, the overwhelming majority of people on the autism/Asperger's continuum do not lie customarily nor manipulate others. I admit this is speculation, but Welles may have learned to lie—with enough aplomb and frequency for the habit to become part of his reputation—in order to get past the wall of resistance the movie moguls were building to imprison his genius.

Did Orson Welles belong on the continuum? Given his early awkwardness, his intense fixations, and his social deficits— all contributing to his major occupational impairment—I believe he did. For all his evident baggage, does he deserve designation as a role model? Again, allowing for his lack of someone's "tough love" when he was orphaned, and considering that he achieved a unique stardom before the movie industry crushed his creativity, I have not the slightest doubt.

In the case of Orson Welles, one must remember that despite his being enigmatic and quirky beyond others' patience, he made incomparable contributions to the performing arts that have been of lasting influence.

Chapter Ten

A Musician/Actor Who Capitalized on Loneliness

Long before Oscar Levant became a typecast actor in movie musicals, I saw him as he intended people to see him—as the leading performer of George Gershwin's concert-level jazz classics such as "Rhapsody in Blue" and "Concerto in F." As a boy I regularly maneuvered someone to take me to Lewisohn Stadium in New York, where I could hear Levant and the Paul Whiteman Orchestra play in annual tribute to Gershwin, who had died in 1937 at age thirty-eight. The ghost of Gershwin created the mood. Whiteman in his signature white jacket and black bow tie established the setting. Levant at the piano gave the concerts their tone, and he gave the outdoor audiences their best memories.

One could say with more than a little accuracy that Levant *lived* to play Gershwin's music. No other performer was able to break the concert-stage barrier against jazz so effectively as Levant. Realizing that no music had ever bridged the chasm

Oscar Levant (1906-1972)

between classical and jazz better than the folk-based works of his idol, Levant pressed hard in order to introduce their purely American sounds to concertgoers.

When Levant was only twelve years old he had seen and heard the twenty-year-old Gershwin play. At home, however, Oscar was forbidden to play popular music. He resolved a number of such pressures by leaving his Pittsburgh home when he was fifteen, heading for New York and musical freedom. By the time he was seventeen, when Gershwin's "Rhapsody" made its debut, Oscar was a leading keyboard interpreter of the Tin Pan Alley songwriter's unique sounds. Later at the piano he out-Gershwined Gershwin, whose huge hands tended to rough over some of the sweeter subtleties he tucked into his works.

Manic-Depressive?

As a refugee from a mother reportedly "inarticulate about expressing affection," Oscar Levant later wisecracked that he felt at home with the brothers Gershwin, George and Ira, because they were "the most undemonstrative people I'd ever met."

Levant's childhood could easily have contributed to definition of the adjective *dysfunctional.* Although biographers have described him as manic-depressive, my reading of his behavior prompts me to match him with *six* of the DSM-IV criteria for Asperger's. Six happen to be two more than necessary for an Asperger's diagnosis, so he very likely belongs on the autism/Asperger's continuum.

Levant was an awkward child, accident prone, and socially inept. "The main characteristic of my youth," he said, "was literalness." When he was told by his watchmaker father to study, he studied, whether they were subjects he found fascinating such as Greek mythology, Jewish ritual, baseball box scores (which he memorized routinely), or any music he read or saw in his head while listening. He seemed able to play with little practice, a talent that few people understood. As I indicated in an earlier chapter, his mother tied him to the piano bench in the mistaken belief such confinement would inspire him to practice more and learn better.

When he was eight, Oscar played in a recital for his extended family. Because young Oscar disobeyed his father by playing an unannounced piece, the senior Levant slapped the boy publicly. The experience changed Oscar's attitude toward performing. He later depended "on an elaborate system of rituals and superstitions just to be able to perform," according to biographers.

The boy wore out music teachers. His older brother observed that after three months with one of them Oscar was ready for another more advanced teacher.

When Levant was twelve the great Polish pianist Ignace Paderewski came to town for a concert. Oscar asked his new teacher, "Do you want to hear what Paderewski is going to play tomorrow night?" His teacher thought the boy was going to tell him the names of the compositions on the program.

Instead young Levant sat down at the piano and played the entire recital for the stunned instructor.

A Truant

At school Oscar pulled poor grades because, by and large, he was not there. He would either be late or skip attending altogether. In his pre-teen years the little rebel took to smoking nickle cigars. His lack of social skills and his awkwardness made him a target of taunting whenever he did show up at school.

For a school's waltz contest, he chose a plain girl as his partner. Because the couple was the last to remain on the dance floor as the music ended, they thought they had won. When the pair stepped up to receive an award, however, the teacher handed them each a lemon—to everyone else's amusement. For the rest of his life, Levant would not allow anyone to serve him a lemon.

Oscar's rebellion accelerated when his father failed to attend his *bar mitzvah*. The elder Levant also did not present or send the young man of thirteen a traditional coming-of-age gift.

Not long afterward Oscar's father died. When his mother realized it was necessary to build distance between the boy and "bad influences" in Pittsburgh, she aided his departure for New York. It is conceivable that she saw his unhappy family experiences among those negative influences.

Although popular music and jazz beckoned at the socio-critical end of the Roaring Twenties, Levant continued to place some faith in what was a remarkable talent for classical music. He even played in New York for the touring Paderewski, who commented, "He doesn't have the soul of a concert pianist."

One career disappointment after another drove Levant into "fitful depression," according to his chroniclers, as well as occasional head-banging and drug addiction. Yet it was as an interpreter of the music of George Gershwin, as a natural and self-deprecating wit, and as an encyclopedic source of trivia that Levant was able to stay afloat in the difficult and unstable environments of entertainment.

Finds a Role

Levant supplemented concert appearances by working in radio, in the movies, and later in television. His was a personality that capitalized not only on a generally sorry condition of mind but on a surprising gift for one-liners when required. Oscar Levant found a niche as an actor, portraying a target of teasing. The shots aimed at Levant were written into scripts on the understanding that, at some point in the plot, he would provide necessary interlude by transforming himself into a momentarily serious and marvelous musician. That, of course, served the Hollywood myth that the nourishment of true genius and talent relied upon acute suffering.

Levant's candidacy for placement on the autism/Asperger's continuum merits six stars because of his profound awkwardness, failure at peer relationships, lack of clear social reciprocity, nonfunctional routines, obsessive practices such as memorizing baseball box scores and details of Greek mythology, and both social and occupational impairment of near disastrous proportions.

Playwright S.N. Behrman observed that Levant was "a character who, if he did not exist, could not be imagined."

I present Oscar Levant as a role model because he possessed marvelous and uniquely contributory talent. And that talent remained intact despite some of the worst emotional hardships a person can endure. He was a thoroughly natural pianist and musician. In the sense that he dignified popular music and jazz at the level of the concert hall, he was a pioneering genius. Having personally seen and heard him at his best, I am thankful for what he gave us.

Levant contributed significantly to American culture by spreading the native sound and beauty of its early Twentieth Century music to concert stages and beyond—all despite his being overloaded with behavioral idiosyncrasies.

Chapter Eleven

A Double Nobel Winner Who Shunned Fame

Thanks to a reconstructed episode in a biography of Marie Curie, this chapter gives me an appropriate opportunity to discuss the admirable ethics shown routinely by many Asperger's people. The point is relevant only if one accepts that Marie was on the autism/Asperger's continuum, and I think she was.

Pierre and Marie Curie—in a scene described by their daughter Eve, who was not born until two years after it took place—received a special postal delivery from Buffalo, New York, one Sunday morning in 1902 at their Paris flat. Eve could only have heard this account from her mother. Pierre was killed in 1906 by a dray, or horse-drawn truck.

Evidently the letter inquired whether the Curies planned to patent their technique for extracting radium from pitchblende or whether they would release the notes of their work "without reserve." Radium treatment was fast becoming the medical

Marie Curie (1867-1934)

profession's cure of choice for malignant tumors. The element was highly marketable.

Pierre broached the subject after reading the letter and described the alternatives to his wife. According to their daughter's account, Marie replied that keeping the rights would be "impossible." Eve said that her mother added, "It would be contrary to the scientific spirit." The Curies chose continuing poverty instead of fortune from royalties.

In that context one must wonder: Perhaps we have traveled backwards in the past century. Many research scientists and their employers seem so bent on cornering future profit potential that we no longer have in our ready consciousness that which Marie Curie referred to as "the scientific spirit."

An Ethic in Decline

The Curies' decision fits an ethic in steep decline today. The fact that the couple debated it at all shows such matters were at a crossroads as the Industrial Revolution began to crest. A century before, Thomas Jefferson unhesitatingly released notes and his design of an improved plow that farmers still use in parts of the world today. He sought to benefit growers struggling with old-style plows. His government positions raised conflicts, however, relative to his applying for a patent. As a lawyer he might have set up a trust for royalty income, but he did not. At the end of his life he was broke.

When faced with such choices, what governs the reasoning of people with Asperger's traits? Remember, they adhere strictly to rules, take statements literally, think in "either-or" terms, do not understand gray areas or ambiguities, have a rigid sense of right versus wrong, and are seldom known to lie. In games at school, teammates criticized my son Fred for blowing advantages and helping the other side. "I had to," he explained to me. "We were winning, and I felt sorry for them."

Reviewing a situation like that, many neurotypical people will have second thoughts about the "right" thing to do. What constitutes good sportsmanship and what does not? Might a player, baffled by the social context of sports, be motivated toward quirky behavior simply to do a good deed?

Asperger's people reason differently—and they follow a traditional and not-totally-extinct brand of ethics. We should be thankful to be blessed by their example.

Today some of us compromise ethics that were formerly second-nature to us all. We do that mainly for monetary advantage, to raise our social status, to boost our sense of power, to feed our vanity, which in turn calms our insecurities. In central Illinois I lived very near the thoroughly self-reliant Amish, who isolate themselves from the mainstream. They respond to human vanity by reminding us, "Self-pride stinks."

Fixated and Childlike

Born Manya Sklodowska in Poland in 1867, the woman we know as Marie Curie had problems of awkwardness that vexed her, was "noticeably" deficient in emotional reciprocity (as an adult, "undemonstrative with her own children"), was strongly fixated and described as obsessed, and was unable socially and professionally to integrate herself into realms of celebrity and personal gain.

"She did not know how to be famous," wrote daughter Eve. Her mother had won two Nobel Prizes, one in physics that she shared with her husband Pierre in 1903, and one in chemistry in 1911. Marie Curie had no notion of exploiting the stature they gave her.

Manya, or Marie, was able to read at the age of four and possessed an "amazing memory." She grew to express "disgust with her own clumsiness." She developed no sense of clothes-consciousness. Many people were struck by her delicate, childlike appearance.

As a scholar Manya had an "innate power of concentration" so strong that nothing—no summoning nor deliberate noisemaking nor other attempted distraction—could draw her attention. Often she appeared obsessed with details of her work. Contemporaries said she had no detectable sense of humor and took everything "deadly seriously, starting with herself." In her teens she would fall ill, "suddenly collapse physically in times of great strain," according to one account. There was not only a suspected "deeper disorder" but the family's simply stated view of her condition—"nervous troubles."

As for family influences, her mother was a gifted pianist and vocalist, and her father taught physics and mathematics. Because the Sklodowskas were in modest circumstances thanks to her father's bad investments, Manya gave up an opportunity for advanced study temporarily to help her sister Bronia go first to study medicine. Then she took her turn.

Positive Idealist

Manya Sklodowska, later Marie Curie, thought of herself as a "positive idealist." Positivism, a school of French thought in that period, tied itself to science and facts, steering clear of values as something lying outside the scientific province. To add "idealist" was an act of social optimism. Manya was uncomfortable with Poland's absorption into the Russian empire. Through clandestine efforts as a young adult she worked to extend educational parity to Polish women. After moving to Paris to study, she met Pierre Curie, in whom she found a soulmate, an "introverted dreamer" like herself. She became "Marie" when they married in 1895.

Dr. Marie Curie made a triumphant tour of the United States in 1921, accompanied by her daughters Irene and Eve and welcomed by President Warren G. Harding. Irene Joliot-Curie was later to win fame as a physicist, and Eve became an author and one of her mother's biographers. Marie's work in accumulating intense radioactive sources proved critical to subsequent research in nuclear physics as well as to the development of medical treatments for cancer.

Marie lectured in several countries and was appointed a member of the International Commission on Intellectual Cooperation by the Council of the League of Nations, forerunner of the United Nations. A Curie Foundation was established in Paris and a Radium Institute in Warsaw, her sister Bronia becoming director of the latter.

Curie's enduring influence upon later nuclear physicists and chemists has been without parallel. Personal sacrifice was to be one of her most memorable characteristics, for she died in 1934 of leukemia brought on by exposure to radium and radiation.

As a person of unflagging persistence and high principles, Marie Curie offers the example to Asperger's young people of a relevant role model. She appeared to have little appreciation for her own importance. She demonstrated—through unique intelligence, through extraordinary focusing, and by her "scientific spirit"—that service to humankind is an honorable calling with or without earthly reward.

In some ways as important as her scientific achievements, perhaps, is a lesson we now draw from her life: Despite a person's having traits manifested by odd behavior, that person may be capable of making extraordinary contributions to society.

Chapter Twelve

A Singer/Actor Who Fought Too Hard

The *Diagnostic and Statistical Manual, Fourth Edition,* on which psychiatric, pediatric, and psychological professionals base judgments of the presence of Asperger's Syndrome, contains a single constant—that the condition results in "clinically significant impairment" in either social or occupational areas.

A person may also be evaluated by selections from multiple possibilities, as outlined and summarized in Chapter Five, but the only constant is the one covering work or social impairment.

More than any other person studied for this book, Paul Robeson, acclaimed bass-baritone singer of African-American spirituals and folk songs from all cultures, leading actor in plays by Eugene O'Neill and William Shakespeare, hits the button hard on the sole criterion that is a constant for

Paul Robeson (1898-1976)

diagnosis—the one covering occupational impairment. While it is true that Orson Welles endured the stifling of his creative genius, he did find employment through his twilight years. Not so with Robeson.

One could say with fairness and accuracy that Robeson sent his own career into a tailspin. He had become fixated, intensely preoccupied (another criterion), with social and political issues. Often he used the concert stage as a platform for his views, to the dismay of most of the audience members. That his bookings fell off should have come as no surprise, but Robeson believed so strongly in his side of the issues that he failed to understand the practical effect of his persuading only a small minority of people. In other words, he lacked a reciprocity of understanding the social effect of his preaching. By itself, such a deficit might not hold in an evaluation for Asperger's—until we learn that Paul Robeson had serious problems with emotional reciprocity (another criterion). He was frank to say of his son, "I have no fatherly instincts about him at all."

On the Continuum

To place Paul Robeson squarely on the autism/Asperger's continuum, we must acknowledge his having met only one more of the DSM-IV criteria. His repeatedly reported failure to nurture age-appropriate peer relationships is that fourth factor, yet there is at least suspicion of a fifth which I will discuss shortly. Robeson's frequent withdrawals—perhaps for study, perhaps to brood—undoubtedly contributed to his difficulty in understanding and acknowledging the way society as a whole perceived him.

Beginning in the volatile 1930s and over the long term, Robeson ignored or simply could not gauge the effect of his outspokenness in behalf of the underdog. A person of obvious "either-or" reasoning, he had no cause to question or doubt the validity of his views. But he appeared to operate on a plane above practical concern for what such championing of the oppressed people of the world would do to his career.

Martin Duberman, his major biographer, described him as "early habituated to solitude," that he had a "penchant for remaining somewhat apart." Robeson exhibited throughout all of his schooling "a loner's temperament" and "the melancholy of confirmed apartness." He was "able to retreat at will to an inner monastic fortress."

Was race involved in such withdrawal, perhaps to flee or hide from signs of prejudice? Not likely, for the record of Robeson's early practice days on the Rutgers University football field show an evenhanded ability to cope with such experiences. He was big enough and powerful enough physically to give back more pounding than he received, and that is what he did. Throughout life, in numerous confrontations over race and his ideology, he was famously quick to scold.

Robeson's persistent and self-imposed periods of isolation from peers, family, and associates were more closely linked with traits of autism and Asperger's, for like Thomas Jefferson he enjoyed studying in splendid solitude. And furthermore, like Jefferson, he gave of himself to others on *his* terms, seldom in proportion to others' needs.

Raised by His Father

The son of a former slave who became a Presbyterian minister, Robeson was an African-American not of poverty but of modest means. His father, the Rev. William Robeson, was solely responsible for raising him after his mother died in a home fire accident when he was five.

Reverend Robeson recognized the boy's gifts and urged him to memorize speeches, whether religious or secular, whether dramatic or drawn from history. He hoped to overcome his son's shyness, a quality that the biographer Duberman touched on with his observation that Paul "did everything well, but preferred to keep in the background." The family atmosphere was devout and dedicated to learning. There is no doubt the honing of Paul's speaking skills helped move him later into the theater.

At Rutgers the young scholar was also an outstanding athlete, achieving All-American status in football and lettering in several other sports. Although popular among students he continued to keep to himself, and by that studious isolation he was able to attain one of the most outstanding academic records in the history of the university.

Were there in Robeson's behavior any signs of yet another of the DSM-IV criteria? I believe there were. I have watched him both on film and in person, and in 1947 I interviewed him in person. My take on the matter is that he was slightly impaired in the area of nonverbal expression. His eye contact was not always steady but was darting in periods when he seemed a bit "wired" or eager to inform others about little-known phenomena. During such periods he had a tendency to go on and on about obscure details without recognizing the effect that such deliveries were having on listeners. Furthermore, as the son of a minister he seldom *discussed* topics but more typically *sermonized.*

While singing, Robeson customarily cupped his hand behind his left ear. It was an embarrassingly awkward gesture, but one that the singer could argue on the facts was necessary to augment his hearing the piano accompaniment more precisely. It did not appear to be an affectation, for he had size, power, voice range, modulating skills, and a bit of charm going for him and needed no such punctuating feature. Still, it seemed incongruous to audiences with the overall style and appearance of this performer who possessed a rich, deep, colorful voice.

From Law to Theater

After Robeson graduated from Rutgers he studied law at Columbia University. The law profession offered sorely limited opportunities to minorities in the 1920s, so he turned to the stage. Taking part in O'Neill's *All God's Chillun Got Wings,* and later playing the title role in O'Neill's *Emperor Jones* in 1924, first in New York and then in London, he inspired wide approval as a gifted actor.

Robeson soon launched a series of concerts featuring spirituals. He achieved widespread recognition for playing the role of Joe, singing "Ol' Man River," in Jerome Kern's 1927 Broadway musical, *Show Boat.* In 1930 he went on to fill the title role in *Othello* in London, a role he reprised on Broadway in 1943. The show set a record for the number of performances of a Shakespearean play in the realm of New York theater.

In the course of his 1930s travels as singer and actor, Robeson visited the Soviet Union and embraced the notion of economic egalitarianism. He entertained American volunteers who were fighting to preserve the monarchic republic during the Spanish Civil War. Meanwhile, from every corner of the world he harvested for concert performances those folk songs that he believed would inspire brotherhood.

Over time Robeson became increasingly vocal about racism, poverty, and workers' interests. Few in his concert audiences welcomed his comments from the stage. To put it more bluntly, most people who went to hear him sing resented his lectures on the plight of the oppressed. Ironically, concert audiences enjoyed the protest songs such oppression gave rise to, but did not understand the long-term responses Robeson hoped to inspire.

Wartime Ballads

The singer/actor maintained a high profile in patriotic performances which bolstered Allied efforts in World War II. He rendered unforgettable tributes to American principles and the ideals of the Founders in such music as "The House I Live In" and "Ballad for Americans."

During general postwar nervousness about increasing influence of the Soviets and their ideology throughout the world, the mood of the country changed—but not Robeson's. He continued supporting ideals considered both foreign and hostile and was often accused of disloyalty. Not only had his acting opportunities begun to dry up in the Cold War, but invitations to perform in concerts dwindled as well. Adding to his woes, the State Department revoked his passport, so he could not perform abroad. After several years the passport was restored, but his voice had begun to lose its luster.

Today the past treatment of Robeson is condemned as unjust by many looking back, some of them the very representatives of agencies who once participated in shunning him. Probably he will be remembered longer as a performer than as an activist. As brilliant and eloquent as he was, he may not have had a soapbox to mount without his great and attention-winning stage talents.

Robeson was a kind man, in many ways a gentle giant, but mid-Twentieth-Century America was not ready to host his passions. In spite of the manner in which he squandered his career, yielding to fixations having little to do with his art, we look back upon his having set standards for dramatic and musical excellence at levels yet to be equaled.

Chapter Thirteen

A Recluse Who Failed Exams and Changed Science

Parents of children with Asperger's Syndrome may be moving beyond such concerns as school grades and intelligence quotient scores. At any rate, that is my earnest hope. As you read this chapter about Gregor Mendel, the father of genetics, and other chapters toward the close of this book, you will understand the basis for my biased optimism.

"My son doesn't test well," other parents have told me on a few occasions. "My daughter is bright—very bright—and she reads or studies all the time. But she just doesn't seem able to raise her test scores."

So where is the problem? Does it lie with test designers who fail to take into account diverse approaches to the material? That could be true with respect to subcultural issues, but it is not the problem here. Does some kind of special malaise set in for the neurologically challenged at test time? Perhaps.

Gregor Mendel (1822-1884)

More than likely we are dealing with a test-taker's anxiety, arising from what he or she sees as slanted test-question language—wording crafted on the assumption there has been uniformity of learning among all who will take the test. The written product of that assumption is a formalism of language for which *freelance* scholars are unprepared.

Many with Asperger's learn better on their own rather than as members of a classroom audience focusing upon an instructor. They will need guidance over what to study in order to complete the requirements of the course, but they may not require the lectures. Dr. Asperger found this to be true and included observations on this point in his landmark study in the 1940s. Among his findings was the realization that high-functioning autistic children seldom learn through the ear. They advance with greater certainty when they can study at their own pace—under the conditions of quiet solitude so many of them apparently prefer.

That habit may be one of the reasons for the common observation that they are loners. They are not necessarily brooding during the entire time they are by themselves. They may simply be reading or reasoning—and thus learning—in the quiet way that is so characteristic of them.

Great Disappointment

I was not surprised to read that the botanist and great experimenter, Gregor Mendel, had precisely the same problems when he failed in 1850, and again in 1856, to qualify for his teaching certificate. In view of what he accomplished for biological sciences, one could say his test anxieties and failure to pass the certification tests did not matter. He did teach after all, but as an uncertified substitute. By Mendel's view the loss was both an openly vexing frustration and a great disappointment.

As a matter of fact, a biographer described Mendel's first failure as "spectacular, the way a train wreck is spectacular," and for Mendel it resulted in an acute sense of shame. On the second examination attempt, he abandoned the effort on the very first question. The problem lay in his being essentially self-taught. Formal references in the test questions threw him off as so much jargon. He had learned his science in a more direct and hands-on manner.

When Gregor Mendel was coming of age in Moravia, young men of promise often chose a monastic life as a means of receiving good schooling and a subsidized education. Mendel had grown up in a struggling farm family, with no means of providing him the education warranted by intellectual gifts that were obvious to other family members. He joined (for life) the Augustinian order in Brno, a large city now part of the Czech Republic. The monastery there attracted studious candidates for the brotherhood of monks, many of whom later became philosophers, mathematicians, mineralogists, and botanists.

When still a serious boy at home, unsuited for the heavy work of farming, Mendel seemed to fall ill at times most inconvenient to those needing help. His illnesses are believed to have been "emotional."

The diagnostic criteria for Asperger's, standards that are very much in flux, do not detail the nonverbal factors resulting in impairments but state them in deliberately general terms. The matrix, however, neither accepts nor rules out the possible presence of persistent tics that may move from one part of the body to another, allergy-like signs that come and go and also shift, real ailments like headaches and diarrhea that anxieties seem to induce, and maladies that appear psychosomatic.

Examination of biographical literature has stirred my suspicions in those areas. Particularly if it seems recurring, perhaps chronic, the presence of those conditions in individuals with a full complement of Asperger's symptoms is persuasive. I believe the professionals reviewing such matters should consider freshening the nonverbal list in the diagnostic criteria by factoring in such socially impairing afflictions.

Slavish Recordkeeper

As for Mendel's meeting the necessary criteria in other ways, there are reports of useful routines carried to extremes of overfocusing. There are also reports of pointless preoccupations that crossed the line and became fixations as well. To finish the match, placing Mendel on the continuum, his thwarted certification ambition stands as a major work impairment, despite extraordinary garden/laboratory success, only because he fretted over the elusive certificate so much.

Asked to record weather data daily and send monthly reports to the Vienna Meteorological Institute, Mendel fell to the task three times a day, also compiling averages and trends to send along with the monthly data reports. He continued the practice without letup for twenty-seven years, almost to the day he died.

For no truly explainable purpose other than to pass the time, however, Mendel regularly scribbled lists having nothing to do with monastic responsibilities or with scientific interests. The copying from directories of common surnames by the hundreds—then arranging, alphabetizing, and rearranging them in searches for name derivations and patterns—is an example of "encompassing preoccupation" while he held a new role as abbot of the monastery. He accepted that appointment with great misgivings because it forced him to surrender serious scientific work.

A Single-Minded Scholar

In the glory days of his scientific efforts, Mendel established the principle that traits pass from parents to offspring in all species by units of heredity now known as genes. In doing so, the trait-carrying units obey generally predictable, mathematical patterns. Mendel went on to expand his research in related areas of genetics, and he presented papers describing his research and findings to the Natural Science Society.

Fellow monks and the people of Brno remained unaware of the enormity of Mendel's discoveries. They knew little about the impact that the findings of this studious monk would have on the general understanding of evolution and on such fields as physiology and medicine. His closest friends complained that Mendel could be so "single-minded" in study and experiments that they lost patience with him. He projected a strong sense of wishing to maintain his privacy, even while he wore what a biographer has called "a veneer of warmth."

At great ease when not focusing on his garden peas or other experiments, Mendel had a sharp wit. His sense of humor at times included practical joking. He often described his having abandoned, at the behest of the bishop, the study of small laboratory animals and turning to garden peas for his experiments. "You see," as Mendel told it, "the bishop did not understand that plants also have sex."

A delightful story involves a monk named Clemens, who walked in the garden with Mendel toward one winter's end, the snow still on the ground. The pair stood before the garden's beehives, whose occupants were venturing for the first time into a warming sunlight. Mendel urged his companion to place his "biretta" or monk's cap on the snow in front of the hives. As the cap lay there, the astonished Brother Clemens watched it turn from black to yellow. The bees, by natural cleanliness, had refrained from voiding inside the hives through winter. In relief they did so by turns on the nearest visible target.

This good-humored monk, Gregor Mendel, despite his carrying traits from the autism/Asperger's continuum, achieved great advances for science. The impact of his vital contributions continues to reverberate in the biological research community and will for some time to come.

Chapter Fourteen

A Collector Who Spiced Classical Music

In another life (a cliché with which an Asperger's person would have difficulty), I taught journalism at McNeese State in Lake Charles, Louisiana. The college had an outstanding fine arts program. As often as possible, I attended recitals and admired the performers' level of musicianship. A music professor sat at the piano during one such program and announced he would play a selection by Bela Bartok.

What followed stunned me for its harshness. I thought it was awful. The crashing, bouncing, and persistent dissonance assaulting my ears made me wish I had chosen something else to do that afternoon. I wondered at the professor's choice of a performance piece, and I wondered even more at those in the recital room who applauded with apparent enthusiasm. In the development of my musical tastes over the years, had I missed something? Or was this composition just plain terrible?

Bela Bartok (1881-1945)

Now that I have read about Bartok and believe I understand him, the piece I heard that day has a contextual relationship for me. I am relieved not to be the only one who disliked his early experimental pieces. Granted that piano composition—and a number of other modern works of noise and disturbing dissonance—may have some worth musically, but no one should feel compelled to explain to me what that value might be.

Bartok suffered two great disappointments early in his career, and it is a wonder—and a benefit to music lovers everywhere—that he did not throw it all aside to go into another line of work. The first defeat was his failure to win a 1905 competition for piano performance in Paris that he was counting on winning. He gave up the notion of becoming a virtuoso and devoted more attention to composing. But the new sounds of his compositions provoked a storm of criticism that Bartok found unbearable.

The Folk Collection

To the good fortune of our music-loving civilization, Bela Bartok fixated upon possibilities arising from an incident that had shortly preceded his Paris disappointment. In 1904 he had heard a servant girl in Transylvania sing a melody so fresh and original that he wrote it down on the spot, noticing its basis was not the standard western scale. With the double loss of virtuoso hopes and of critical approval for his compositions, he turned obsessively onto a new and exciting path that the girl's song had pointed toward.

Bartok began collecting folk music from obscure corners of his native Hungary and from neighboring Romania, later from other Balkan areas. At times in the company of fellow Hungarian composer Zoltan Kodaly, who had an equal passion for folk tunes, Bartok used what was in those days a unique method. With a wax cylinder to record the songs of the peasants and workers, he directed them to sing into a huge, cumbersome horn he carried all over the countryside. In his search he lived in peasants' homes and enjoyed their hospitality, later remarking this period of his life had given him his happiest memories.

Eventually, Bartok moved on to collect nearly 6,000 folk melodies on three continents and became the world's leading advocate of the delights of folk music.

That shift, seen by chroniclers of his life as an obsession, proved his salvation as a music professional. His arrangements and his later compositions incorporating native melodies now stand as his most tuneful and popular works.

More importantly, Bartok influenced serious classical music lovers in many parts of the world toward appreciating more fully the quality and value of their own folk music. A staunch Hungarian national since early adulthood, Bartok emigrated to the United States in 1940 when his remaining in a Hitler-dominated Europe became unsafe.

Bartok also served as a teacher and lecturer, roles he continued in this country during his final years. He wrote and edited books on Hungarian, Romanian, Yugoslav, and Slovakian music. He inspired music conductors to expand their repertoire and give greater performance stature to works considered strongly ethnic.

A Prodigy

Bela's mother was a music teacher. The boy showed an interest and an ear for music at age three. He accompanied his mother's piano playing by beating the rhythms on a little drum. By the time he was four he had memorized the distinct patterns of dozens of folk tunes in that manner. When he was five, Bartok begged—"keeping on at (his parents) continually"—for piano lessons. He showed great aptitude, and at nine he wrote a waltz entitled "The Course of the Danube." He performed that work publicly at age eleven to local acclaim.

"Learning, always learning," was the way his mother described effects of Bela's routines. He played no games with other children or anyone. One schoolmate remarked Bartok "struck anyone who met him only once (by) the way he looked at one," adding that at times a "mystical, fanatical flame burned in his eyes."

After the debut performance of his waltz, news of Bela's gifts prompted an offer of more concentrated music instruction, to which his now widowed mother consented. Serious in all things, Bartok focused with greater intensity as his opportunities for music studies increased.

Biographers have also described Bartok as "self-contained," introspective, and showing in his writings a "meticulous adherence to facts." His passion for collecting included tangible folk objects, which he always arranged "in systematic order." Yet about his personal appearance he seemed somewhat unconcerned. He was attached to a "threadbare brown overcoat," although he could afford better. There are references also to his having been socially awkward, a "man of limited conversation," and possessing a "probing, combative nature."

The Academy of Music in Vienna accepted Bartok upon his application, but he chose instead to study at the academy in Budapest to be with his friend (and later composer) Erno Dohnanyi. Despite the comradeship of young men with musical talents, Bela maintained the serious reserve that even his mother had found remarkable.

Refused to Accept a Prize

Several separate descriptions point to failures of socially appropriate peer relationships, to circumscribed preoccupations, and possible early perseverating. There are reports passed along by his mother of a few pointless routines, and there is strong likelihood that the description of a "combative nature" was a sign that Bela lacked the know-how for appropriate social reciprocity.

One additional anecdote helps paint a more vivid picture of general social impairment, and the point will add weight to Bela

Bartok's candidacy for placement on the autism/Asperger's continuum:

When he was a mature performer and composer of forty-five, he participated in a competition promising a prestigious reward, a prize considered to be an important honor in European music circles at the time. Bartok won the competition. However, upon his examining the text of the citation that accompanied the prize, Bartok found errors in references to some of his compositions. He was so incensed by the imperfect citation that he refused the prize.

Notwithstanding quirks of personality, Bela Bartok held generous views toward humankind. "My guiding idea," he wrote at midlife, "which I have been conscious of ever since I found myself a composer, is the idea of the brotherhood of nations, a brotherhood in spite of war and strife. This is the idea I am trying to serve, with the best of my ability, in my music." The fixated, enigmatic composer contributed significantly toward appreciation by those nations of their respective folk cultures, and it was that common bond of native expression that Bartok hoped would unite them in brotherhood.

Chapter Fifteen

A Stargazer with Otherworldly Beliefs

My noticing similarities of life experiences among the people I researched for this book has been a surprise. I am not referring essentially to similar symptoms of Asperger's traits among them. Rather I refer to comparable behavior and experiences that seem almost to sprout from common roots. Later, I will illustrate with several parallels.

For now, as examples that are relevant because you have read this far, I offer descriptions and ask you to identify—

- A person awkward in youth, largely self-taught, amazingly precocious, somewhat pedantic, primarily a loner, and confused at times between reality and fantasy.

- Or, a troublemaker at school, annoyingly egotistical, a youth who played piano to acclaim at Carnegie Hall and whose mother was obnoxiously irrational.

Carl Sagan (1934-1996)

- Or, a boy conforming with his parents' wishes and possessing great memorization skills, very competitive in sports, and, as an adult, standoffish with his offspring.

In the first instance you might conclude I was describing Thomas Jefferson. In the second you might hazard a guess at Oscar Levant. In the third a likely choice might be Paul Robeson. Actually these descriptions—*all* of them, and some of them classic Asperger's traits—fit Carl Sagan alone, the man who brought astronomy and outer space into pop culture.

Bundle of Contradictions

People who watched his guest shots on the Johnny Carson program probably had insufficient perspective to conclude Sagan was a bundle of contradictions. One of his biographers referred to his having a "dual nature." The writer said Sagan as a child was aware of this two-sidedness—his inclination to withdraw from others and devote time to his interests, offset by a "strong competitive streak like his mother's" that drove him to excel in street games.

In another description from childhood, Sagan is said to have received a particularly difficult assignment in Hebrew school as a consequence of his propensity to give the teachers fits. The penalty/assignment, however, "played to his competitive instincts," driving him to plunge in and master the work for no other reason than to prove he could.

At another level, in a description within the context of his first marriage (to a precocious fellow scientist), Sagan's inclination to be a loner was in combat with his "excruciating need for attention." A champion of feminist causes, he was also blatantly sexist, at least in early adulthood.

Professionally he took aim at false claims in the name of science. Yet he regarded the shaky phenomenon of unidentified flying objects as truth and, at least in his youth, suggested that Moses and Jesus had probably arrived on Earth by such means.

Sagan barely won approval for his doctoral dissertation. Harvard denied him teaching tenure. The National Academy of Sciences would not admit him as a member, but it presented him an award for popularizing science. Nevertheless, he presented a relatively unglamorous subject, astronomy, to the public in ways that gave it sex appeal. Even at that, Sagan's beaming science into the living room for the edification of common folks did not prevent his regarding "most people" as his intellectual inferiors, at times telling them such "cruel truths" in face-to-face encounters.

Extraterrestrial Life

Sagan's mother was a talented writer but reportedly "paranoid," "neurotic," "irrational," and "insane," by various descriptions. The boy was quite attached to his father, whose family emigrated from Czarist Russia and was successful in the garment business. A budding intellectual, Sam Sagan, Carl's father, had hoped to attend Columbia. Family needs pulled Sam into the factory when his own father died.

Carl showed signs of fixations as early as five, when for some unknown reason he decided to write consecutive numbers on shirt boards from one to a thousand. The significance of that lies not in the fixation so much as in the age-inappropriate achievement. Throughout school, particularly in high school, much of what he learned he absorbed from reading on his own, not from lectures.

Sagan developed an early fixation about life on other planets. The subject was one of such consuming interest that he drove himself quickly to a faith in the reality of UFOs. He arrived at his theory of the origins of Moses and Jesus when he was seventeen. It is safe to add that nobody ever proved him wrong—nor did Sagan ever try seriously to prove his contention right. Interestingly, I have heard young people with Asperger's Syndrome describe high school experiences with teachers and peers as a sign they had landed on "the wrong planet."

Observations by Sagan in his book, *Cosmos* (the title also of a television series he hosted), open widely the forms he believed life might be taking elsewhere in this solar system. He is probably the first popular writer outside the science fiction genre to have argued convincingly that extraterrestrial life need not resemble ours in substance, general shape, locomotion, or any other way. He called clearer attention to effects of differences among planetary systems in potential life support, thus his theorizing of "balloon" beings on Jupiter.

Earthly Understanding

Even more helpful at a practical level was the informed guidance Sagan gave unmanned space missions to Mars and Venus. His insights into the origins of life on Earth were also edifying and stemmed from his interest in possible bases for extraterrestrial life. He gave a critical demonstration: Sagan showed how irradiating a mix of methane, ammonia, and hydrogen sulfide gas could produce amino acids—a building block of life. To true believers in science, such a laboratory challenge to creationist theory was inevitable but never intended to shake the foundations of faith.

Social impairments persisted throughout Sagan's life. He never wore a watch, so he was notoriously late for appointments. He argued publicly with those who disagreed with him. By various accounts, however, he either mellowed near the end of his life or simply rose to occasions by putting aside, selectively, his combativeness, bad manners, and emotional reserve.

My placing Carl Sagan on the autism/Asperger's continuum seemed an easy task because he left so many footprints. As with Orson Welles, it was difficult for me to decide whether to like him.

Whenever we hold up a role model for anyone, a general cantankerousness may show through. That is the part we prefer young people to resist copying. But can we get that point across to those with Asperger's who may take us literally over the words "role model"? I honestly think we can.

We can reason with youngsters by cautioning them, "By the way, about this person, there's something you should know...." Our children are not idiots. They know right from wrong. When any of our selected geniuses has a reputation for having acted like a spoiled brat, we should be frank about that.

The overriding point is that such quirky and often outlandish behavior did not diminish Sagan's significant contributions. And a generous corollary to his abrasive manner might be, "Well, maybe he had his reasons."

Chapter Sixteen

A Performer Who Seemed Wedded to His Piano

Only one of the achievers I chose for this book, Canadian pianist Glenn Gould, was the subject of a professional, published evaluation of his idioysncratic behavior, but it was posthumous. Dr. Peter Ostwald, psychiatrist and the pianist's friend and biographer, speculated that Gould may have had Asperger's.

Gould was the greatest interpreter of the keyboard music of Johann Sebastian Bach in modern times. He died of a stroke at the age of fifty in 1982. That was years before Asperger's Syndrome was generally understood on this side of the Atlantic.

Dr. Ostwald authored *Glenn Gould: The Ecstasy and Tragedy of Genius*, published in 1997. He died the year before his book about Gould came into print. Rejecting the possibility that the pianist had infantile autism, Dr. Ostwald

Glenn Gould (1932-1982)

noted that some of Gould's childhood and adolescent behavior, which he described as—

> a marked fear of certain physical objects, disturbances in empathy, social withdrawal, self-isolation, and obsessive attention to ritualized behavior—does resemble a condition called Asperger Disease...occasionally associated with an unusual degree of giftedness in...music, mathematics, drama, athletics, or art.

In addition to the writings of neurologist Dr. Oliver Sacks, whom Ostwald cited, he probably also checked his copy of the DSM-IV, published by his own professional association. However, Ostwald wrote as "disease" what the manual refers to as "disorder," what most professionals prefer to call "syndrome," and what I generally give a slightly more neutral reference, "condition."

Disliked the Color Yellow

Gould appears to have had sensory problems associated with light, temperature, and possibly the sound of voices. "I hate the sunlight," he said. As though the color signified brightness for him, he added, "I hate yellow." His biographer analyzed as a social issue Gould's habit of overdressing, not as a sensory issue. Yet it could have been both social and sensory, for he feared catching colds. "The envelope of heavy clothing he wore," Ostwald wrote, "was like a cocoon, sealing him from human contact."

Similarly the pianist felt "edgy" when two other people were in the room with him, and three or more "caused his social anxiety to escalate sharply." Thomas Jefferson did not have the confinement portion of this problem, but he wrote that he was uncomfortable when two or more in a room spoke simultaneously. For such reasons as that, Jefferson met with cabinet members singly. He banned political conversation at the dinner table. The effect of voices may have been the same for Gould.

Remember that Hans Asperger wrote it was possible for high-functioning autistics to be both hypersensitive and hyposensitive. Within that realm the pianist's performing with a large symphony orchestra would have been acceptable in ways that mixed speaking voices would not.

Issues of awkwardness arise commonly in descriptions of Gould, especially in settings where large groups would notice—the pianist's stage performances. One writer called attention to a "disconcerting strangeness" in Gould's concert behavior, mentioning posture. That included the way Gould walked, stood, and sat. His head was almost at the level of the keyboard.

Ostwald discussed that same peculiarity of piano playing, and he also mentioned an awkward stride. Gould cast a "hesitant and unfocused" gaze toward his audiences. Moreover, he had a tic, "some mild twitching of the muscles," close to his right eye. Describing his subject's early

126

years, the psychiatrist/biographer judged him, whether by temperament or awkwardness, "totally unfit for any sport." The pianist never married.

Shield of Humming

Along with these liabilities, Gould had some social assets. He had a "very boyish quality about him," possessed a droll sense of humor and would often do impersonations, spoke with a "joyous discharge of emotion and intellect," and carried a strong fixation "in defense of animals." The boy had absolute pitch at the age of three. His father noted, "When you'd expect a child to cry, Glenn would always hum." Recalling Jefferson, humming was *his* anxiety-reducing activity of choice.

Public performance so filled Gould with anxieties that he retired in 1964 after only nine years of concerts to work solely in recording studios. He claimed the move was partly to experiment with recording technology, a field in which he was well-read. Yet he also revealed that "at live concerts I feel demeaned, like a vaudevillian."

Gould was fanatical about guarding against cold germs. He washed his hands obsessively and was fixated on drugs and the practice of medicine, in which field he considered himself something of an expert. He made a point of "telling the doctor what to do rather than listening to his opinions," according to Ostwald. Doctor's office visits would often end in arguments.

Very Self-Directed

Robert Fulford, author and the Goulds' next-door neighbor, wrote—

> Even as a child Glenn was isolated because he was working like hell to be a great man. He had a tremendous feeling and loving affection for music.... It was an utter, complete feeling. He knew who he was and where he was going.

Gould's parents were musicians. He was three generations removed from Norwegian composer Edvard Grieg. Until he was ten his mother (described as "a little on the cold side" and slighted in Gould's later descriptions of her) was his only piano teacher. The boy had a "phenomenal musical memory."

Glenn began composing at five and played his compositions for friends and family. At ten he entered the Royal Conservatory of Music in Toronto. Although he won an important music competition at twelve, it was to be his last because he developed a dislike for competition of any kind, especially among musicians. He was awarded a diploma with highest honors from the Conservatory when he was fourteen.

Gould adopted his strange, signature piano posture, including his use of a "rickety folding chair," when he was a young teenage performer.

Because he became so well-known as a virtuoso pianist, Gould is largely unappreciated as a writer, composer, conductor, broadcaster, and sound technologist.

Significant to the point of identifying Glenn Gould as possibly having had Asperger's Syndrome are signs of his perseverating style in conversation. "Words flowed out of him with unabashed vitality, making it difficult to interrupt," Ostwald wrote. And in a later reference—

> Speech flowed out ceaselessly and seamlessly, under great inner pressure. His vocal exuberance seemed like some kind of primal experience, a joyous discharge of emotion and intellect, mockery and fantasy, all designed to fascinate if not dominate the listener. At no time did he ask what my thoughts and reactions might be....

My observations in *Diagnosing Jefferson* include a one-sided incuriosity about others' thoughts and similarly seamless vocal outpourings in the second half of Jefferson's life.

A pithy and perhaps valuable observation about the public perception of Gould appears in an anonymous biographical sketch available on the Internet: "What some have considered strange was, in fact, only different." That idiosyncratic difference, however, certainly did not rob Glenn Gould of the chance to pursue his dream of greatness as an unparalleled performer and interpreter of music.

Chapter Seventeen

A Lyrical Messenger—
An American Original

John Hartford was an admirer of Thomas Jefferson. He knew Jefferson had been considered one of the finest violin players of his time until a wrist fracture shut that down. Observers described Hartford's own focusing on fiddle playing as "extreme." Such seeming intensity in combination with other factors led me to theorize there was an association with Asperger's—in at least a mild form.

Some will say Hartford's general sociability rules out a match with the traits of Asperger's. Although he suffered from non-Hodgkin's lymphoma for more than two decades, declining to shake people's hands for fear the squeeze would break his fingers, Hartford managed to hide his distress much of the time. He was affable and witty. He pushed himself physically to perform for his friends and audiences when probably he would rather have rested. When interacting with anyone for any

John Hartford (1937-2001)

reason, Hartford maintained an air that belied all apprehensions about his cancer.

Unless one keeps pace with evolving diagnostic criteria, especially those affecting seasoned adults, such sociability might seem to make an exception of Hartford. Actually, "qualitative impairment in social interaction," as a feature of DSM-IV criteria, is an observational guideline aimed largely at studying children or unintegrated adults. It says nothing of occupationally successful adults, to whom I will return in a moment.

Limited Uniformity

Reason dictates that an autism spectrum would apply in the social area as in other diagnostic areas. Some with the condition will do better socially than others. Dr. Attwood, in *Asperger's Syndrome*, cites four standards of diagnostic criteria at the start of his chapter titled "Social Behavior." It becomes obvious there is limited uniformity in what is an evolving standard for diagnosis. In fact, in his words:

> As we develop our knowledge of the unusual aspects of the social behaviour associated with Asperger's Syndrome, the diagnostic criteria will become more precise. At this stage much of that knowledge is based on clinical impressions rather than rigorous scientific study.

Returning to Thomas Jefferson, while it is true he had many friends, there is much evidence those relationships were one-sided. His brilliance and charisma attracted others to him, and in matters of friendship Jefferson was a bit egocentric.

Coincidentally, the Text Revision of the DSM-IV, issued in 2000, says older people with the condition "may have an interest in friendship" without understanding the rules of interaction. Any deficit in social exchange is "more typically manifest by an eccentric and one-sided social approach to others." The DSM-IV-TR adds, perhaps surprisingly for many, that such behavior is a nearly complete opposite of "social or emotional indifference."

The autistic savant and author Jerry Newport, featured on CBS's *60 Minutes*, and the human resources manager and Asperger's speaker Jean-Paul Bovee are both outgoing and chatty. In that regard they defy stereotyping of their condition. The same observation of social skill applies to Hartford, never diagnosed with Asperger's. Whether learned or natural, however, the social successes of Newport and Bovee have never overturned their Asperger's diagnoses.

Poor eye-gaze in conversation shows up on all diagnostic scales as a sign of social impairment. But the relatively sociable Newport and Bovee are—and the late John Hartford was—observably unsteady or inconsistent in eye contact. Jefferson also had eye-gaze problems.

Finally on this point we have testimony of adult movement toward sociability from another authority, who added that work success may—or will in fact—lead high-functioning autistics to a measure of social success. The authority asked us to ponder what will happen to many high-functioning children when they grow up. "In the vast majority of cases work performance can be excellent, and with this comes social integration," Dr. Hans Asperger wrote in his original study nearly sixty years ago.

"Gentle on My Mind"

Hartford won his greatest public attention and acclaim as the composer/lyricist of "Gentle on My Mind" in the mid-1960s. The song depicts a wanderer who is saddened by a stay-at-home loved one. In four stanzas ending similarly, the wanderer wants freedom from "bonds," yet he hints that he may return. He expands his independence by scorning others' judgments, broadens his ranging, tells of running from a conquest with "tears of joy." Finally, cast with hoboes, he honors his eternal anchor with a poetic vision of her "wavin' from the backroads, by the rivers of my memory," and remaining ever "gentle on my mind."

Hartford captured wide attention after Glen Campbell and others recorded that song. The Smothers Brothers booked him for their show regularly. He even hosted his own show briefly. Offered a starring role in a detective series, he turned CBS down and returned to Nashville, where his music earned him three Grammy awards. He was a prolific composer and performer in bluegrass and traditional music, alternating his fiddling by playing guitar and banjo among other instruments. His performances were eccentric. His compositions and lyrics were offbeat. The singer Johnny Cash was inspired to comment about Hartford, "He has his own world."

Hartford's fellow artists considered him a perfectionist in musical efforts. He carried index cards to make notes of projects running through his head.

Fascinated also by the riverboats he saw cruising the Mississippi when he was growing up in St. Louis, Hartford worked and studied to obtain a riverboat operator's license. His home just outside Nashville overlooked the Cumberland, where he watched river traffic and often joined it as a ship's pilot. One of the books he authored, *Steamboat in a Cornfield* (Crown, 1986), dealt with a historic riverboat.

Common Characteristics

Besides violin-playing and their relative ease of attracting friends, John Hartford and Thomas Jefferson shared as other interests and characteristics–

- the design of their homes, the main portion of Hartford's resembling a steamboat's interior,

- exceptional talents for storytelling,

- a love of dancing (Hartford would dance while fiddling or picking a banjo),

- a penchant for collecting books ("up to the ceiling" as Hartford described it in the documentary *Down From the Mountain*, a reprise by musicians who had performed for the movie *O Brother, Where Art Thou?*),

- a talent for drawing and design, including Hartford's unique flourish of double-handed calligraphy while signing autographs,

- an unconcern the two shared with Albert Einstein for letting their hair go uncombed (a minor social deficit that Jefferson's portrait painters corrected),

- the passing up of a significant moneymaking opportunity (Hartford's spurning CBS, and Jefferson's donating his inventions to posterity without patent),

- facial tics in Hartford and vocal tics in Jefferson (the latter humming under his breath constantly, even while he read),

- and the previously mentioned specific-to-general assembling of details in order to arrive at general principles.

With regard to the last, Jefferson showed that best while taking over half a century to piece together Monticello. Hartford revealed it in his personal philosophy. He told of trying—during performances—to fiddle a fine-detailing of music he would "hear" in his head. He compared that to an artist's trying to paint a better picture—concerned less about the result than the grand effect of individual colors the picture required.

Despite his popularity, Hartford regarded himself as a mediocre musician. No doubt that was why he devoted so many hours daily to practicing on the fiddle.

My placing John Hartford on the Asperger's continuum answers yet another logical consideration: Often in assembling a number of characteristics and attempting to explain them, no other explanation presents itself so clearly as Asperger's Syndrome.

My judgment about Hartford was triggered generally by his riverboat and other fixations. For example, as a young man he interviewed banjoist Earl Scruggs, arriving with eight pages of questions about the instrument alone. My selection of Hartford for inclusion in this work was also based in part on his career decision to reject TV series stardom. Our generally avaricious society would classify that as "significant impairment." Because of the diagnostic significance of nonverbal factors, there was also a witnessed eye-gaze problem over a long period for me to take into account.

Hartford appeared to have identified strongly with Jefferson, an interest that, by itself, is worthy of our attention. Whether hero-worship or intellectual fixating, the choice suggests that behind John Hartford's cheerful nature dwelled an enigma of which he was aware—indistinct, yet more soothing than troubling.

Once more we have a personality from the past—this time the very recent past—whose idiosyncrasies failed to dampen his success. As an artist, and definitely in his own way, Hartford contributed significantly to the rich tapestry of the American folk scene.

Chapter Eighteen

A Prodigy and Rebel Who Never Grew Up

Wolfgang Amadeus Mozart was unable to mature at pace with his chronological age partly because his family would not let him. There is reason to doubt young Mozart was capable of standing on his own successfully. From birth he exhibited developmental differences. He was born with a head too large for his delicate body. Eighteenth-Century Austrians were quick to regard his phenomenal musical gifts as signs of a miracle. In the Twenty-First Century we are still uncertain about the basis for savant skills, but we are at least looking into it.

Mozart required the care that one would give a boy whose body matures faster than his temperament. As he grew, however, he was determined to free himself, to get a grasp on adulthood. That was a hope he could not manage well. Finally, struck by a rare, pervasive skin disease, the greatest of musical prodigies went to a pauper's grave in Vienna on a dank

Wolfgang Amadeus Mozart (1756-1791)

December day in 1791—at age thirty-five. His wife did not attend the burial, nor was anyone else present to mourn his passing.

Mozart's story is either one of exploitation by an ambitious father or one of overprotection by a *caring* father— or a little of both. Leopold Mozart saw profit in the boy's genius, but did opportunism alone drive him to manage precocious Wolfgang? Can we fix blame justly on Leopold for his son's fitful rebellions and eventual misfortunes?

All signposts point to Mozart's belonging on the autism/ Asperger's continuum: reported awkwardness, inappropriate responses during anxiety, fixations in composition and in performing musical tricks (such as endless theme variations), his savant skills, his self-distancing from realities, and classic social impairments. According to a contemporary observation by an acquaintance, Adolph Heinrich von Schlichtengroll:

> He never knew how properly to conduct himself. The management of domestic affairs, the proper use of money, the judicious selection of pleasures, and temperance in the enjoyment of them, were never virtues to his taste. The gratification of the moment was always uppermost with him.

Acute Memory, Incredible Genius

At three, Wolfgang delighted in experimenting with melodies at the harpsichord. When he was four his father, a court musician in the Archbishopric of Salzburg, began to give him lessons. He noticed that the boy's musical aptitude seemed instinctive. Wolfgang at practice sensed what was right or wrong without anyone's correcting him. His hearing was so sensitive he knew when a violin string was tuned an eighth of a tone off. Once at a trumpet blast he fainted with pain.

Young Mozart had a memory so acute he could reproduce music without error after hearing it once. He could improvise a theme for half an hour without repeating himself. He played pieces at first sight-reading as competently as others who had practiced them for hours. At five Wolfgang became a serious composer of minuets, moving on to sonatas at seven and a symphony when he was eight.

Leopold Mozart decided when the boy was six to begin exhibiting Wolfgang's talents. The family began a three-year tour. Young Mozart played for the crowned heads of Europe. He charmed all from Vienna through Paris, Brussels, The Hague, London, and back, giving countless performances in major cities between. He continued to compose as he traveled.

"Everyone is amazed," Leopold wrote home of Wolfgang's reception on one of the early tours, adding that many people had observed that "his genius is incomprehensible." The rewards of the tour performances were often spontaneous gifts and sums of money. Such appreciation for the unusual amusement amounted to many times the salary that the elder Mozart had received as a court musician.

After a few years of young Mozart's extraordinary success, the enthusiasm by European nobility for the touring prodigy began to wane. As a pre-teenager, Wolfgang was no longer cute. In fact, some artists rebelled against performing in operas the youngster had been commissioned to write. They believed it was beneath them to sing or play music written by a mere boy. The glory days for the Mozart family came to a halt.

New Sponsor

Because young Mozart soon came under sponsorship of a new Archbishop in Salzburg who was unimpressed with the boy's genius, life grew comparatively dull. His appeals for adequate subsidy became impassioned. Regardless of his continuing to compose what amounted to masterpieces for the court, he received little or no recognition and found further association with Salzburg stifling. Approaching the size and years of young manhood, Wolfgang wanted to get away.

Leopold had begun to take note of the fact that his remarkable son's responses to others were becoming idiosyncratic—that people now regarded him as awkward and strange. While he had dreaded Wolfgang's coming of age because of what it would mean to the family income, Leopold now sought to keep his son in check because he observed Wolfgang's "helplessness and childishness." He refused to let the young man travel with any adults other than family members.

At twenty-one, accompanied by his mother, Wolfgang visited Mannheim and fell in love with Aloysia Weber. Promptly he made plans to run off with Fraulein Weber to Italy. But in this, as in Wolfgang's other love affairs, his father interfered by feverish correspondence. Young Mozart and his mother moved on to Paris, where he took a joyless job as organist at Versailles. His mother died the following year, in 1778. Finding himself alone, Wolfgang set out for Mannheim where, this time, Aloysia barely knew who he was.

Young Mozart then returned to his drab role in the Salzburg court of the unappreciative Archbishop Hieronymus von Colloredo. A fierce argument between them in 1781 drove Wolfgang to rebel. He fled both the church and his father's domination.

Vienna and Salieri

By nature Wolfgang seldom brooded but was optimistic about his prospects. Moving to Vienna, where some influential people remembered him well, he soon received deserved recognition as both a pianist and composer. Emperor Joseph II commissioned him to write a new opera, *The Abduction from the Seraglio.* A jealous competitor, Antonio Salieri, tried to block its production. Failing that, Salieri sent hecklers to the scheduled performance, but they cheered instead.

Flush with excitement over his operatic triumph, Wolfgang Amadeus Mozart made plans for a bright future. He decided to wed Aloysia's sister, Constanze Weber. Leopold thought her unsuitable, but his open objections did not deter the couple.

The young composer adapted nicely to his new life and repeated operatic successes, despite Salieri's renewed pranks against *The Marriage of Figaro*. Again the plot to ruin young Mozart backfired, this time owing to the enthusiasm of the cast that had been told falsely the music was unsingable.

Finally and quickly, however, a doggedly jealous Salieri staged an opera of his own, so catchy that it drew attention from Mozart's new achievement. The result was disastrous. After only nine performances, *The Marriage of Figaro* was withdrawn from the stage. The short run had yielded Mozart too little to pay his debts.

Although Wolfgang Amadeus Mozart followed other opportunities and was commissioned to write *The Magic Flute*, illness was beginning to consume him. The prospect of death was on his mind. He approached the writing of "Requiem" with a sense of foreboding. The work had been commissioned by a mysterious stranger who had come to his door (actually the representative of a notorious musical plagiarist, not Salieri as some believed). The ailing Mozart referred to the piece as "my funeral song."

Shallow Gratifications

Reports of Mozart's perpetual optimism and cheerful disposition may appear too bright an application to a life of such highs and lows. Contemporary reports persist, however, that Wolfgang was affable and that he continued to love life with a passion despite all setbacks. He also loved dancing, and he loved nice clothes. Above all he loved being the center of attention. Comforting in small respects, those positive but shallow virtues fell short of assuring his survival in a harsh world.

Offsetting the more joyful observations of Mozart's general nature are those insisting he was too immature not to remain in the guardianship of a responsible adult, such as that of his father Leopold. The elder Mozart died four years before Wolfgang's untimely death in 1791.

The widow Constanze Mozart might have set matters in better balance after she remarried. As the wife of Mozart biographer Georg Nissen, she pleaded martyrdom at the hands of a thoughtless genius. The part that she evidently got right, however, was that the genius remained a child until the day he died.

The reflected genius of his work and his legacy endure. Many musicologists regard Wolfgang Amadeus Mozart as the preeminent composer of Western Civilization. That is a broadly shared view of a man who was also, very likely, the most enigmatic of musician/composers ever to put hands to a keyboard.

Chapter Nineteen

Surprising and Strange Parallels

In making notes about the lives of these thirteen people, did I notice any patterns of behavior that might be significant? Aside from their sharing important matches with diagnostic criteria and sharing a number of Asperger's traits, did they handle some of life's choices similarly? And if they did, are there any clues that might tell us why?

As a matter of fact, I ran across several surprisingly common threads. Because I am not a scientist, I have few (if any) reference points for seeing them as anything beyond coincidences. But because I deal in matters having to do with Asperger's Syndrome—uncovering historical figures who showed signs of the condition—their similarities of behavior may represent, in some instances, patterns relating closely to it.

I have not calculated probabilities for the similarities that crop up among the thirteen people I have described.

Furthermore, some links that follow will seem more significant than others.

What I am counting on is that a few shared characteristics—such as responses to the known behavior of parents that led to Oscar Levant's finally heading for New York and Wolfgang Amadeus Mozart's rebellious flight to Vienna—will in time be traceable to the autism/Asperger's spectrum condition they appeared to have in common.

As a further example, consider the fact that all of the subject celebrities were either musical by vocation or avocation or they were scientists—or in a couple of instances they were both. Music and science are two creative fields into which people with Asperger's traits move rather commonly, or they might choose them as sidelines.

Thomas Jefferson was fond of calling himself a scientist, although he was never paid for tinkering in that area. He was also an extremely competent violinist. We have no information whether he tried to play pianos or harpsichords, but we know he could tune them. Pianist Glenn Gould fancied himself to be an amateur physician. Scientists Carl Sagan and Albert Einstein were capable pianists, and Einstein also played the violin.

Musical Families

Parents of seven among the selected role models were musical by occupation or strong commitment. Four of the seven chose musical careers for themselves—Bela Bartok, John

Hartford, Glenn Gould, and Wolfgang Amadeus Mozart, although in the case of Mozart one could say the career chose him. Gould followed *both* parents into music. The others of the seven having a musical parent were Marie Curie, Albert Einstein, and Orson Welles, with Einstein and Welles adding music mastery to their other skills.

There seems nothing extraordinary in this next example, but three had a parent who taught in a field *other* than music. While the celebrity children did not enter schoolteaching as a prime occupation, Paul Robeson, Bela Bartok, and Marie Curie lectured widely in and out of academia. Bartok served as a conservatory-level teacher of music.

By another coincidence, Robeson, Bartok, and Curie, along with Thomas Jefferson and Carl Sagan, expressed strong opinions on public issues. With only slight hesitation I could add Albert Einstein. Madame Curie voiced her Polish nationalism and feminism under guarded circumstances. Jefferson, perhaps the worst public speaker ever to become President of the United States, expressed his views almost exclusively in his writings. Jefferson also had trouble speaking French but could write in that language, and exactly the same pattern was true for Marie Curie.

Charles Darwin weighed the possibility of becoming a physician like his father, but his interests veered away. John Hartford's father was also a physician. If I were to broaden the category to include parents with *scientific* backgrounds, I would also include Marie Curie and Albert Einstein, with Thomas Jefferson's father coming close as a geographer and cartographer.

Five lost a parent during childhood, with Orson Welles losing both of his. The others were Thomas Jefferson, Charles Darwin, Bela Bartok, and Paul Robeson.

But *six* were either severely inhibited or downright unflattering in expressing memories of their *mothers*—Thomas Jefferson, Charles Darwin, Paul Robeson, Glenn Gould, Oscar Levant, and Carl Sagan. Levant was also uncharitable in references to his father.

Withheld Affection

Because problems of emotional reciprocity are so conspicuous in diagnostic criteria for people on the autism/ Asperger's continuum, it should come as no surprise to learn that four of the subject celebrities revealed a marked inability to demonstrate affection toward their children—Paul Robeson, Carl Sagan, Marie Curie, and Thomas Jefferson.

Six of the selected role models were either "childish" or "childlike" according to descriptions by close friends or associates—Mozart, Curie, Gould, Levant, Sagan, and Jefferson—and that characteristic is also consistent with common Asperger's traits of naivete, literalness, and "either-or" reasoning.

At least five of the thirteen persons were unkempt about their appearance, whether in the way they mismanaged their hair, clothing, or both. In some cases their wardrobe choices were strange—Albert Einstein, Thomas Jefferson, and Glenn Gould. In the other two instances, they were just tacky—Marie Curie and Bela Bartok. Wolfgang Amadeus Mozart on the other hand was a dandy, extremely clothes-conscious.

Perhaps a lack of concern about grooming is attributable to their focusing on more important matters. The brilliant achievements of the five who were careless about their general appearance are, after all, the features of their lives we will remember best.

All of my choices were highly intelligent people. Eight of them had, by all accounts, incredible skills of memorization— Carl Sagan, Marie Curie, Paul Robeson, Glenn Gould, Thomas Jefferson, Oscar Levant, Orson Welles, and Wolfgang Amadeus Mozart.

Seven gave signs of one kind or another that they were uncomfortable with the instructional features of formal schooling, preferring to learn on their own—Gregor Mendel, Albert Einstein, Oscar Levant, Carl Sagan, Orson Welles, Charles Darwin, and Thomas Jefferson.

A Matter of Principle

Five of the persons described in this book declined on principle—an ethic that is uncommon and barely understood today—to use their achievements primarily as a means for advancing their financial interest. That is a far cry from practices of, say, pensioned and protected United States ex-presidents, who trade on an already well-rewarded position in order to command colossal speaking fees and whopping book advances.

- As mentioned earlier, Thomas Jefferson declined to patent his inventions (an act that would have netted him royalty payments) because of the government positions he held. Ultimately, he went broke.

- Madame Curie, at a time of great financial need, was emphatic in discussions with her husband that they must decline rewards of personal claim to their discoveries. To her, accepting payment would violate the "scientific spirit."

- Charles Darwin became sick with anxieties by withholding publication of his compelling scientific conclusions. He could muster no enthusiasm for profiting from a challenge to the established view of creationism.

- Bela Bartok refused a prestigious prize that could have enhanced his career opportunities. The prizegivers had not described accurately his achievements for meriting the citation, so he viewed the honor as flawed or tainted.

- John Hartford turned down a leading role in a dramatic network television series—declining such celebrity advancement, by best accounts, because it had little or nothing to do with his musical interests.

Early Achievers

Twelve of the thirteen subject celebrities reached significant watersheds in their careers by the time they were thirty years old. Four of those twelve established vividly the talents or insights associated with their fame before they were twenty.

Only Gregor Mendel proved a late bloomer. His botanical experiments leading to laws of heredity did not begin until he was thirty-three, the same age Jefferson was when he wrote the Declaration of Independence. The relatively precocious twelve, then, starting from oldest to youngest—

- Thomas Jefferson joined defiant Virginia burgesses (his writings for whom underlay the 1776 Declaration) a month before he turned thirty-one.

- Marie Curie discovered the elements polonium and radium (bases for finding radioactivity that led to a Nobel Prize) when she was thirty.

- John Hartford became immortal in American folk/pop music by writing "Gentle on My Mind" when he was twenty-eight.

- Charles Darwin was prepared to share with the world his theory of evolution when he was twenty-seven.

- Paul Robeson reached highest acclaim as a dramatic actor on two continents when he was twenty-six.

- Orson Welles created the motion picture *Citizen Kane* and thus insured his immortality at the age of twenty-five.

- Bela Bartok began combing the Eastern European countryside for folk melodies—his gift numbering thousands of tunes—when he was twenty-three.

- Glenn Gould's renditions of the "Goldberg Variations" won him acclaim as Bach's greatest keyboard interpreter in modern times. He was twenty-two.

- Oscar Levant mastered George Gershwin's piano music (both his life-sustaining interest and his lifetime contribution) when he was seventeen.

- Carl Sagan developed and shared with Washington officials his early theories of extraterrestrial life when he was seventeen.

- Albert Einstein formulated the principles we now refer to as his theory of relativity at the age of sixteen.

- Wolfgang Amadeus Mozart achieved his highest celebrity status as a musician when he was six.

Chapter Twenty

A New Look at
the Concept of Genius

Dr. Temple Grandin has often said and written, "Genius is an abnormality."

The implications of such a statement are far-reaching. There was a time I understood genius to represent one end of what psychologists call a normal distribution curve of intelligence. Dr. Grandin's statement challenges old notions held by parents of bright children, standards of educators who administer or rely on tests, and procedures of professionals in both social and medical sciences.

As a parent who is by no means a scientist, I will try to describe in lay terms the implications of the thesis Temple Grandin presents.

We customarily define genius as an extraordinary capacity for creativity. We refer to autism as the consequence of a brain abnormality. The manifestations might be off-the-norm behavior, high intelligence, low intelligence, or something between. The high level or its opposite could even go off the charts at one end or the other.

To say it is "abnormal" for anyone to possess the creative capacity known as genius may sound radical, *unless* we accept that no two brains are exactly alike in their physical makeup. Is it possible, then, that among geniuses we may be dealing with a spectrum of brain abnormalities?

In other words, for some *not* receiving a genius score on an intelligence quotient (IQ) test but also being moderately creative, relatively bright—might they have brain abnormalities less pronounced than those carried by autistics, particularly by those with Asperger's? I believe it is possible.

IQ Tests in Question?

In the context of Dr. Grandin's statement, we should deal with the IQ tests themselves. Are they to be rendered invalid as measurements? Not exactly, but in terms of what she believes, and for reasons associated with what we know of Asperger's behavior, the validity of such tests comes under serious question.

If we accept that the presence of genius relies on a structural difference in the brain, should we continue to say the tests measure intellectual capacity? Or should we say the results merely reflect the degree of that physical difference?

We should factor in the problem that Asperger's children often test poorly. Something about the language of the test questions suggests a classroom lecturer drafted the questions in a way he or she believed they would be understood by the majority of the test takers. Or the problem may be that the customary literalness of Asperger's people is a block. They are slowed or confused by ambiguities in the questions, each requiring a clear and correct answer, all of that within time limits.

We are also into issues of fairness when some who take the test are not able to fathom fully the meanings of all questions. What is the value of a testing instrument—one that is partly intended to uncover a high potential for creativity—if a person with a high potential for creativity cannot make reliable response to the measurement?

Better Tests, or None at All?

Given what we have learned in a relatively short time about Asperger's Syndrome—its potential for yielding up individuals with extremely high intelligence, some with savant skills, some with remarkable capacities for memorization—should we not be relying on new and more suitable forms of testing?

Or do we even need tests to uncover the capacity of what stands before us in these uniquely creative minds? Why not just say a cheery "Hello!" to such mentally gifted people and give them rein to apply their talents as constructively as they wish, in whatever field they wish?

If we come to realize that so-called intelligence testing may be nonproductive when applied at the suspected high end—

given the possibly discoverable validity of the proposition, "Genius is an abnormality"—we could also begin to doubt the merits of our present forms of intelligence testing generally.

In a society such as the United States, with a national policy of "inclusion" or mainstreaming all its schoolchildren, what is the point of such tests? Is it to give us a standard by which to apply "special education" to those in need? That approach costs money we have resisted spending, a level of funding that taxpayers generally have been unwilling to support, and an area of preparation that fewer and fewer teacher candidates seem willing to enter.

However, if the tax-supported body of public educators ever becomes committed to complying with the Individuals with Disabilities Education Act, there might then be a purpose in testing for intellectual capacity. We would then be compelled not only to know who needs special help, we would also be compelled to provide it.

Acknowledging the Obvious

While it is true that inclusion benefits many children, it does not work for every child. Some who are perpetually distractable or who have short-term memory problems may require individualized instruction or small-group teaching.

We seem wedded to such vague commitments as "leave no child behind" or "no child left behind," which are admirable values but which fail to clarify the teaching methodologies that will help slower children keep up with the faster ones. The standard downplays our allowing special needs students access either to self-contained classrooms for the special attention they require or access to the most appropriate teaching methods that will fit their needs.

We should have no trouble—even without tests—identifying the children for whom inclusion is working and the children for whom it is *not* working.

Those for whom inclusion may not be appropriate are the children who are dropping back academically and shutting themselves away socially. They are behind in their work because they cannot understand it, or they are unequipped to tackle it in the way teachers present it. They retreat to self-isolation because they know they are lagging, and they have few skills for overcoming that lag in order to make friends. Often they are teased by their peers, and that teasing closes off friendly interaction.

Mind you, I am not opposed to well-crafted tests—whether for examining aptitude, verifying giftedness, or objective measurement of skills and academic attainment. By objective, incidentally, I do not necessarily mean administrators' pressure upon teachers to "teach the test," when they know district-by-district comparisons of student skills will be published in the local paper. Such a practice has too little educational value.

The Hazards of Caste

Perhaps owing to the success of people like Bill Gates, society is arriving at a more respectful view of those we may categorize as "nerds," or what we formerly referred to as "grinds" or "bookworms." I applaud the apparent shift in public perceptions.

I have lost patience with adults who—observing a male child who dislikes school, is preoccupied with sports, and is socially charming—will proclaim, "Now there's a real boy!" Or they might say, "He's all boy!" What such adults fail to realize is an implication—that a "nerd" who enjoys studying, has little or no interest in sports, and is socially unskilled becomes, in others' minds, perhaps a fake boy, or a partial boy.

Carrying public perceptions to another level, I believe there is no danger society will ever create a special category of geniuses. I foresee no cornering of the market on inventing whatever needs inventing, creating whatever nonexisting art and music the rest of us might enjoy, or making new scientific breakthroughs to enrich our health and happiness. In that respect this is still an equal opportunity world. Science fiction to the contrary, I see no prospects for an elite of geniuses. The implications run too deep. A society organizing itself along such lines would lose its individual and collective motivations, its adventurousness, its inclination to confront opportunities, and its hopes.

We are fortunate there exists a strong and a natural sense of justice and rule-following in the makeup of many people with Asperger's. Even when abstract concepts are difficult for detail-oriented Asperger's people to grasp, most have a sense that selects right over wrong, selects the broadly ethical over the blatantly opportunistic, the fair over the unfair, the just over the unjust.

I oppose assigning the bulk of creativity to any class of geniuses in a contrived manner, whether they are geniuses who happen to have Asperger's traits or people whose genius seems totally unrelated to neurological differences. Regardless of the routinely reliable instincts by Asperger's people for good versus evil, and regardless of reliable reasoning skills by gifted persons who are neurotypical, I also oppose assigning any such class a dominion over moral judgments.

I oppose the *Brave New World* mentality that Aldous Huxley warned against. The gifted themselves prefer to be free and independent spirits, as an even exchange for their contributing to a society that barely understands them.

Chapter Twenty-One

Our Discomforts
—Their Rights

The possibility that I may be the first writer to give Leopold Mozart the benefit of doubt would surprise me. Definitely it would please me to know that. Instead of his possessing a strong sense of control, indicated by his blocking Wolfgang from living life as the young man wished, Leopold may have acted from overpowering anxiety regarding his son's vulnerabilities. We fathers and mothers of young people who have developmental differences are extremely concerned about that. We know in many respects the world is a jungle, and our Asperger's-affected children are lambs.

At this writing my son Fred, who has just turned eighteen, is in correspondence with a four-year university to which he seeks transfer from his local community college. The prospect of my son's living away independently is terrifying to me, as it must have tortured Leopold. When I now read the elder Mozart's words of two centuries past, I see softness in his heart where others saw iron in his hand.

What, specifically, worries me so? An Asperger's person such as Fred (known to have helped game opponents because he felt sorry for them) could conceivably surrender his spending money to another college student who spots an easy mark. He might lend his car for a falsely crafted "emergency," and perhaps not have it returned when he needs it. Regardless of advice, he is too kindhearted and generous in situations that another person with seasoned social skills might enter skeptically. He is not stupid in such matters, and he insists he would stand firm in his best interests. But he is, as is true of many Asperger's people, entirely too accommodating. Will that prove a flaw, or may it remain a virtue?

While young Mozart maintained a generally cheerful disposition, his father observed that in times of anxiety Wolfgang would become weepy and show a sense of loss. Leopold was concerned because his son in young adulthood continued to exhibit childlike traits. The lad's talents placed him in situations that were, at times, beyond his understanding, because not everyone dealt with him honestly.

The Real World

People with Asperger's who are trained for independent living are beginning to learn the "ways of the world," or, to be truthful, ways in which the world might hurt them. Support groups in which they meet and counsel one another are strongly helpful.

Jerry Newport's book, *Your Life Is Not a Label* (Future Horizons, Inc., 2001), provides important tips about getting along successfully in a world run by neurotypicals who do not always play by the rules. A very popular book by Liane Holliday Willey, *Pretending to be Normal* (Jessica Kingsley Publishers, 1999), describes her experiences in environments far from the comforts of a sheltering family. Oprah Winfrey highlighted *Soon Will Come The Light* (Future Horizons, Inc., 1994) with an appearance on her show by the author, Thomas A. McKean. His work provides insight into the way high-functioning autistics navigate this world.

More and more, the spectrum characteristics of autism are receiving media attention. The condition of Asperger's Syndrome is more widespread than previously thought, or becoming more widespread as a result of environmental factors.

Perhaps parents of Asperger's children leaving the nest are the ones who need counseling. Their support groups almost never confront the topic of "letting go." Customarily the groups focus on horror stories about children's experiences at school. Discussions often revolve around frustrations in trying to win public school compliance with the Individuals with Disabilities Education Act.

Entirely too soon the special-needs children of their concern will be grown and moving out of high school, into college, or going directly into the work force. When they do, separation anxieties will revisit families that have not seen such apprehensions since the youngsters were enrolled in kindergarten. This time, however, the fears will attack parents more keenly than young people, who may see the future as an adventure.

In that respect, Asperger's youths are like all others in late-teenage years. They are more curious about leaving than they are apprehensive. They relish more the freedoms than they weigh the responsibilities. They wonder what life will be like when it can be lived *not* under parental watch. They are, perhaps, savoring such prospects.

What Do We Owe?

This is difficult for an Asperger's parent to write or say, but I must do so emphatically: As vulnerable as youngsters with Asperger's Syndrome may seem to be, they are entitled to carry the support and full confidence of their families when they leave the nest.

Those final days, when parents of Asperger's youngsters are tempted to offer yet another piece of cautionary advice, will be uncomfortable all around. But the moment always arrives when young people have one foot out the door mentally and emotionally. We owe them faith in their ability to make it on their own.

The self-esteem of Asperger's youngsters is tied closely to their wish for relative independence. They want (in many respects they already own) the right to *try*, even at the risk of disappointment and failure. Learning how to handle failure is critical to their progression toward maturity. They will get lumps, but the lumps will heal.

When proposing rules of conduct for a young man, Thomas Jefferson asked rhetorically, "How much pain have cost us the evils which have never happened(?)." My grandfather, David Ledgin, gave that more precision: "Ninety percent of what we worry about never happens." But again, such worries are too burdensome for starry-eyed Asperger's achievers. It is enough that the anxieties are a weight on parents' shoulders.

How Jefferson was able to come up with the phrase "pursuit of happiness" is a topic of never-ending debate among scholars. But it is exactly the opportunity, the hope, and the promise of that pursuit that we owe our children, Asperger's or not. If we fail to show them confidently the course toward that pursuit, they will question the full meaning of those other unalienable rights and entitlements—"life" and "liberty."

The maturing process for bright high-functioning autistics is also one of exciting discovery. How far will their talents carry them? What innovations are they capable of creating, for the benefit of how many people, for what rewards that will gratify them?

They will even consider such a question as this: "To what extent will my achievements bring honor to my supportive and loving family?"

Some parents have a different concept of their immortality than others. Mine has long been tied to the simple notion that I want my children to remember me well. The better-prepared I can make them, and the more readily I can let go and allow them to prove *to themselves* their capabilities, the better everything will go for everyone.

Chapter Twenty-Two

Choosing to Be Gentle on Their Minds

What writers have described as the voice of a "free spirit" has touched me keenly in the lyrics of John Hartford's famous song, "Gentle on My Mind." A parent, teacher, or professional who has helped an Asperger's youngster and now stands on "the backroads by the rivers" of that young person's memory—and is kept as "ever gentle" on his or her mind—is receiving a unique honor.

High-functioning autistics reason differently, and very likely they remember differently. What may be sweet nostalgia to neurotypicals could be something that rests quite dissimilarly in Asperger's people's minds. A memory that is a solitary and unremarkable experience to them may be a richly rewarding and unforgettable moment to the rest of us. *Or the other way around!*

Family members grow apart because of time or distance, especially in a relatively dynamic society such as the United

States. Anyone remembered well as aiding the release of a creative mind is already receiving all that he or she can expect or reasonably hope for. Because of the strong sense of place, routine, and family held by Asperger's youngsters, the luck of good remembrance is on the relative's side and the side of anyone who gave warm friendship, mentoring, or support to such young people.

Either Side of a Line

Some with Asperger's Syndrome will marry, and some will not. Their choices will fall either side of a line that may shift because of studies or work commitments. Some will have children, and some will not. Some will be affectionate toward their children, and some will not.

Some will be generally cheerful in their day-to-day outlook, and some will not. Some will be famous, and some will not. Some will become rich, and some will not. Some will care what others think about what they do, and some will not, charting their paths regardless.

Standing between "normal" or "typical" behavior and Asperger's behavior are issues of emotional reciprocity, social understanding, sensory issues, and values associated with black-and-white, right-or-wrong, and either-or reasoning.

With respect to our Asperger's children, should we dwell on such differences, or should we be glad simply to have been part of their lives? Should we keep hovering in the hope that we can provide safety nets, or should we just let them be? Should we persist in voicing our concerns, or should we be careful not to nag?

Should we celebrate their triumphs and cheer them past their defeats with appropriate parental pride and optimism? Or should we observe what they are trying to make of it all and then follow their lead by joyful expression or reserved acceptance?

Realizing we can never appreciate completely what we have in an Asperger's son or daughter—that we must simply be glad we gave this person to the world—should we not just love him or her no matter what, and pretty much let it go at that?

Chapter Twenty-Three

Parents as Role Models

In addition to the heroes and heroines of history whose achievements were remarkable, despite their odd traits (in a few cases *because* of their differences), we must place parents of young people with Asperger's Syndrome in the role-model picture.

How prominently? Actually, in a vital and very basic way, Mom and Dad may be the most important role models of all.

Any parent's silent acceptance of role modeling, along with the likes of Jefferson and Einstein, would be relevant on a few planes:

A father or mother is well-positioned to put forth a set of values—whether by verbalizing, by example, or both—on which a youngster affected by Asperger's will base rules of conduct for the rest of his or her life.

High-functioning autistic people respond to rules quickly and follow them rigidly. However, someone in a position of trust must delineate and define those rules and move on to explain why modern society hopes everyone will live by them.

Although we may be comfortable saying these young people have an *innate* sense of right and wrong, that sense is closer to being a quick, defensive perception of what this strange environment expects. After all, neurotypicals set common-denominator standards for society. Asperger's people are pre-programmed to follow the beat of a different drummer, and early on they recognize that difference. At times, whether as teenagers or older, they may have the same problems as neurotypical people.

We all trust that *parents* of Asperger's people will provide their young with context, the everyday application of rules. For spelling out the rules, parents should not shift responsibility to teachers, clergymen, or the justice system.

Explaining Conflicting Values

In the standards of some cultures, it may be "right" to do something our Westernized society would frown upon. Given the Internet and worldwide reporting of events, Asperger's youngsters will hear about such exceptions. Well, nobody said parenting was an easy job. Mom and Dad must be ready to explain why some people accustom themselves to one set of values, and others in this world choose to walk a separate path.

Procedures for successful social interaction require parental guidance because an Asperger's person will not recognize those steps by simple observation. Classic features of Asperger's Syndrome are an inability to read facial expressions and body language and an inability to interpret social chit-chat filled with puzzling and emotion-laden abstractions.

The parental job of leading a fact-oriented and very literal youngster through the mine field of social jargon—helping him or her process the full intent behind such expressions as "Way to go, man!" and a zillion other rhetorical gems—can be quite a challenge, ranging in outcome from rewarding to maddening.

Another plane on which the parent has the advantage over a historical figure is that of informed hindsight. The parent may reinforce positive behavior in such ways as this: "Patience, unselfishness, and family loyalty are lessons we can learn from the life of Marie Curie."

Turning the coin, the parent may combat negative inclinations: "For all his genius, Carl Sagan's high-and-mighty arrogance (or Orson Welles's, or Albert Einstein's) was quite unfair to people who loved and tried to help him." How about this one for the youngster who speeds through his allowance as though there is no tomorrow?: "Let me tell you about Thomas Jefferson's habit of living beyond his means and how costly that was to his family." There is no reason our children cannot learn from these celebrities' mistakes.

The parent is at once a teacher and mentor in such situations. The very fact that he or she is engaged in that way at all is a hallmark of role modeling. Among the most satisfying observations I have ever heard—and I have heard them frequently from Asperger's teens and young adults—are ways Mom or Dad stood by them in times of stress, believed in them, guided their special qualities, and kept faith in their potential for unique success.

Talented Asperger's parents sometimes mentor youngsters outside their own families because of their special work in the adult world that young people, autistic or not, find fascinating. A number of parents of Asperger's children have become quite innovative in constructing social situations from which their offspring will ultimately learn and benefit.

Siblings of Asperger's children join frequently in helping their brothers or sisters make their way more smoothly, reducing tensions common in a somewhat forbidding environment. It is because of their understanding of the condition that siblings may also, ultimately, bond with other Asperger's people outside the famly whom they get to know and grow to admire. Sound future professional or business alliances—even marriage partnerships—could lie ahead from that kind of special relationship.

Other Living Role Models

Because professionals are better acquainted with Asperger's Syndrome today than they were, say, a decade ago, it is now possible to observe traits in living, prominent people with fair accuracy. In that connection the man probably destined to be named the most philanthropic in the history of the human race, Bill Gates, is high on the list of the formally undiagnosed who are suspected of Asperger's tendencies. A PBS series early in 2002 called "The Secret Life of the Brain" placed Gates alongside Dr. Temple Grandin in a spectrum of thinkers.

Mention was made earlier in this book of Dr. Grandin as a role model. I have observed huge audiences of neurotypicals rise in acclaim for her insightful presentations. She brings to countless parents and teachers knowledge of autism and hope for the future of their charges.

Less prominent in the public eye but helpful nonetheless is a growing legion of new Asperger's-affected authors of personal accounts. They are frank to disclose their past fears and failures as well as their present determination and success, each one of them now a living role model.

Parents can set the tone—the model—for special rearing of Asperger's children by reading such accounts, attending conferences and listening to speakers, joining support groups, discussing issues affecting these young people, and asking questions.

Because school is an environment loaded with hazards to the self-esteem of Asperger's young people, parents must focus on learning the ins and outs of the so-called IEP process— Individualized Educational Programs that are provided for in the IDEA—Individuals with Disabilities Education Act. A parent's participation in that process will provide a quick study of who in the school really cares about the child.

At times one must find the "emergency exit" for the youngster–and one is available through the GED program– General Education Development. If high school seems a trap from an Asperger's teen's point of view, the GED is a splendid option. Accommodations for diagnosed people are available to those taking that test.

More than what parents say, whatever parents *do*–whether learning more about their children's condition, becoming advocates at school, even in such everyday practices as driving a car or commenting on news of the day or saying "please" or "thank you" with regularity–the children *watch*.

For that reason parents must dip into their enormous reservoirs of patience and self-examination skills in order to equip Asperger's youngsters by deed as well as by word. Parents are, in that sense, the example–front and center as role models.

What About His or Her Future?

One thing is clear about tomorrow, and that is that it will come whether we are ready for it or not. All parents will look back and question whether they did everything it was reasonable to do in order to prepare children with Asperger's Syndrome for the future. Parents of neurotypical children worry as well, but probably not to the same extent.

A point I have made in this book is that these youngsters in our temporary care are a talented, creative, but sensitive lot. Only within the past ten years have we begun to see development of primers for teaching them social skills to avoid pitfalls of life in a world managed by neurotypicals.

Only recently have we begun to understand the careers Asperger's people might prefer or become competent in, whether by virtue of fixations or inclinations associated with their condition or, perhaps, governed to an extent by their social inhibitions. The fascinating world of computers, for example, is one that satisfies several of their comfort requirements.

If parents connect often as loving Moms or Dads to ease their children's way on this planet, those children will not go through life wishing the stork had delivered them to a different one.

When youngsters start asserting their autonomy, parents must meet them halfway or farther and always be crystal clear and very frank about what needs saying.

Will parents make mistakes and have regrets? Are they destined to do things they will wish they had never done, fail to do things they wish they *had* done? Parents are doomed to look back and believe they might have done their jobs better. Conscience guarantees parents such a fate.

But parents of Asperger's youngsters should take comfort in this thought, as I do: They have each given a remarkable person to a civilization that needs him or her, because our society is still developing and trying to find its way. I am absolutely confident our Asperger's offspring will be of extraordinary help.

Appendix

Asperger's Traits That Make Us Happy

Asperger's Syndrome is described most frequently in terms of deficits—low social skills, awkwardness, etc. However, we should recognize many positives. The teacher cited in the dedication has suggested a brief presentation of these traits:

A person with Asperger's Syndrome is likely to—

- Display a dependable commitment to honesty and truth,
- Offer to be helpful and accommodating,
- Be a reliable keeper of promises,
- Show strong ties to home and family,
- Obey rules and persons in positions of authority,
- Be creative in several interest areas,
- Exhibit a natural sense of fairness and justice,
- Resist compromising his or her principles,
- Have an appealingly droll sense of humor,
- Set high standards for his or her own work,
- Be organized and get things done,
- Inspire confidence by virtue of intelligence and reserve.

Sources

Books

American Psychiatric Association, *Diagnostic and Statistical Manual of Mental Disorders, Fourth Edition*. Washington, D.C.: American Psychiatric Association, 1994. *Text Revision*, 2000.

Attwood, Tony. *Asperger's Syndrome: A Guide for Parents and Professionals*. London: Jessica Kingsley Publishers, 1998.

Autism and Asperger's Syndrome, Uta Frith, editor. Cambridge, U.K.: Cambridge University Press, 1991.

Brady, Frank. *Citizen Welles*. New York: Charles Scribner's Sons, 1989.

Brian, Denis. *Einstein: A Life*. New York: John Wiley & Sons, Inc., 1996.

Cross, Milton, and Ewen, David. *The Milton Cross New Encyclopedia of the Great Composers and Their Music* (two volumes). Garden City, N.Y.: Doubleday & Co., Inc., 1953.

Curie, Eve. *Madame Curie*. Garden City, N.Y.: Garden City Publishing Co., Inc., 1943.

Davidson, Keay. *Carl Sagan: A Life*. New York: John Wiley & Sons, Inc., 1999.

Desmond, Adrian, and Moore, James. *Darwin: The Life of a Tormented Evolutionist*. New York: Warner Books, 1991.

Duberman, Martin Bauml. *Paul Robeson*. New York: Alfred A. Knopf, 1988.

Ellis, Joseph J. *American Sphinx: The Character of Thomas Jefferson.* New York: Alfred A. Knopf, 1997.

Grandin, Temple. *Thinking in Pictures–and Other Reports from My Life with Autism.* New York: Doubleday, 1995.

Henig, Robin Marantz. *The Monk in the Garden: The Lost and Found Genius of Gregor Mendel, the Father of Genetics.* Boston: Houghton Mifflin Company, 2000.

Jefferson, Thomas. *Writings,* Merrill D. Peterson, editor. New York: The Library of America, 1984.

Kashner, Sam, and Schoenberger, Nancy. *A Talent for Genius: The Life and Times of Oscar Levant.* New York: Villard Books, 1994.

Ledgin, Norm. *Diagnosing Jefferson: Evidence of a Condition that Guided His Beliefs, Behavior, and Personal Associations.* Arlington, Tex.: Future Horizons, Inc., 2000.

Lesznai, Lajos. *Bartok.* London: J.M. Dent & Sons, Ltd., The Master Musicians Series, 1961.

Levant, Oscar. *A Smattering of Ignorance.* Garden City, N.Y.: Garden City Publishing Co., Inc., 1942.

Malone, Dumas. *Jefferson and His Time* (six volumes). Boston: Little, Brown and Company, 1948-81.

McKean, Thomas A. *Soon Will Come The Light: A View from Inside the Autism Puzzle.* Arlington, Tex.: Future Horizons, Inc., second edition, 1996.

Myles, Brenda Smith, and Simpson, Richard L. *Asperger Syndrome: A Guide for Educators and Parents.* Austin, Tex.: Pro-Ed, Inc., 1998.

Newport, Jerry. *Your Life is Not a Label.* Arlington, Tex.: Future Horizons, Inc., 2001.

Orel, Vitezslav. *Mendel.* Oxford, U.K.: Oxford University Press, 1984.

Ostwald, Peter. *Glenn Gould: The Ecstasy and Tragedy of Genius.* New York: W.W. Norton & Company, Inc., 1997.

Pflaum, Rosalynd. *Grand Obsession: Madame Curie and Her World.* New York: Doubleday, 1989.

Poundstone, William. *Carl Sagan: A Life in the Cosmos.* New York: Henry Holt and Company, 1999.

Solomon, Maynard. *Mozart.* New York: HarperCollins Publishers, Inc., 1995.

Thomson, David. *Rosebud: The Story of Orson Welles.* New York: Alfred A. Knopf, 1996.

White, Michael, and Gribbin, John. *Darwin: A Life in Science.* New York: Dutton, 1995.

Willey, Liane Holliday. *Pretending to be Normal: Living with Asperger's Syndrome.* London: Jessica Kingsley Publishers, 1999.

Articles

Brennan, Sandra. "John Hartford: Biography." RollingStone.com, June 9, 2001.

Dansby, Andrew. "John Hartford Dies." RollingStone.com, June 5, 2001.

de Toth, June. "Bela Bartok: The Early Years." GeoCities.com.

———————— "Bela Bartok: The Traditional Years." GeoCities.com.

Glasstone, Samuel. "Albert Einstein." Microsoft Encarta Online Encyclopedia, 2001.

"Glenn Gould Biography." GlennGould.com. Sony Music Canada.

Golden, Frederic. "Person of the Century: Albert Einstein." Time.com.

Graham, Bill. "Bluegrass pioneer will remain gentle on our minds." *The Kansas City Star,* June 17, 2001.

Ledgin, Norman. "Paul Robeson Sees World Understanding Via Education in Post-Concert Targum Interview." *The Targum,* Rutgers University, January 10, 1947.

Ledgin, Stephanie P. "John Hartford: Back & Forth In Time." *Sing Out!* Vol. 45, No. 2. Summer, 2001.

Osborne, Lawrence. "The Little Professor Syndrome." *The New York Times Magazine,* June 18, 2000.

Roberts, Dalton. "Hartford remains gentle on the mind." *Chattanooga Times Free Press,* June 15, 2001.

Strauss, Neil. "John Hartford, Composer of Country Hits, Dies at 63." *The New York Times,* June 6, 2001.

www.ingramcontent.com/pod-product-compliance
Lightning Source LLC
Jackson TN
JSHW011936131224
75386JS00041B/1411